WITHDRAWN

Bullying from Streets to Schools

Bullying from Streets to Schools

Information for Those Who Care

Page A. Smith and
W. Sean Kearney

ROWMAN & LITTLEFIELD
Lanham • Boulder • New York • London

Published by Rowman & Littlefield
A wholly owned subsidiary of The Rowman & Littlefield Publishing Group, Inc.
4501 Forbes Boulevard, Suite 200, Lanham, Maryland 20706
www.rowman.com

Unit A, Whitacre Mews, 26-34 Stannary Street, London SE11 4AB

British Library Cataloguing in Publication Information Available

Library of Congress Cataloging-in-Publication Data Available

ISBN 978-1-4758-2623-4 (cloth : alk. paper)
ISBN 978-1-4758-2624-1 (pbk. : alk. paper)
ISBN 978-1-4758-2625-8 (electronic)

∞™ The paper used in this publication meets the minimum requirements of
American National Standard for Information Sciences—Permanence of Paper
for Printed Library Materials, ANSI/NISO Z39.48-1992.

Printed in the United States of America

To the two Rons—Etter and Poulton—
whose expertise, tenacity, encouragement, and empathy
keep both bullies and life from burying me up to my axles
—Page

To all those who have been impacted by bullying and
to the brave individuals who stand up for the powerless
—Sean

Contents

Acknowledgments

We acknowledge and thank both Sarah Jubar, our editor, and her colleagues at Rowman & Littlefield. However precarious her choice to enlist us, Sarah is a professional of the first rank and a wonderful person. Her patience is truly humbling, and she is a credit to the industry.

Foreword

Bullying seems to be woven into the fabric of some people's DNA. We have all witnessed or been the victims of it. Bullying knows no social or economic bounds: it can affect anyone from the young Prince Charles, heir to the British throne, bullied in boarding schools, to Chiron, the young, poor boy so tormented in scenes from *Moonlight*. Bullying manifests itself in different forms—emotional, verbal, physical, relational, and cyber—characterized by the imbalance of physical or social power. It no longer only occurs face-to-face. The digital age has created opportunities for individuals to be bullied remotely, repeatedly, and anonymously.

Although bullying can occur in any context in which humans interact with each other, here Page A. Smith and W. Sean Kearney focus on bullying in the context of interactions in schools. They argue that it is a substantial and growing problem, one that teachers, administrators, and other school personnel encounter far too often—and not only between students, but also between adults in school organizations. They translate what research tells us about bullying into an informative, practical guide for those interested in not only understanding it but also being proactive to reduce bullying and its impact on victims and others.

In clarifying misconceptions about bullies and helping us understand underlying motives for their behavior, Smith and Kearney provide valuable insights for school professionals, parents, families, community leaders, and others interested in reducing such behavior and the emotional trauma and violence it breeds. But the authors go well beyond helping readers understand bullying—they provide concrete suggestions for how schools, religious groups, community organizations, and families, as well as the police and social service organizations, can combat bullying by reinforcing social community norms and refusing to tolerate bullying behavior. They urge us to uphold a belief in the value and integrity of every individual by not being passive bystanders. The research-based strategies they provide, as well as their recommendations for school leaders, teachers, and students, make this a must-read for all members of the school community, as well as all those interested in being proactive in reducing this increasing problem.

Dr. Michael DiPaola
Chancellor Professor
Department of Educational Policy, Planning, and Leadership
College of William and Mary

Introduction

Bullying represents a very serious problem. By all accounts, the effects of bullying on victims, bystanders, and bullies themselves derail the best efforts to educate children and maintain school civility. This book reduces the academic "glare" often associated with translating research into practical and workable knowledge for those interested in curbing bullying. It presents information about bullying in an understandable format designed for school stakeholders, community agents, parents, and students.

Strangely enough, we begin our book on bullying by introducing you to the finer points of fishing. Specifically, we parallel the artistry of trout fishing with the earnestness applied to eliminating bullying by people who care.

Avid anglers generally acknowledge trout fishing as the sport's ultimate challenge. To be sure, there are a multitude of hopeful participants involved in tossing lines, tippets, and flies toward watery pockets presumed to hold nature's "aquatic royalty." However, as many discover, things are not as easy as they seem, and very few fishermen seeking a prize cutthroat, rainbow, or brown trout are consistently successful in transferring fish to net.

Indeed, the scant few anglers who enjoy the successful bend of the rod are keenly aware of the streamside environment they are exploring, the equipment involved in increasing their odds of a catch, and the attention to detail necessary to locate the most wary of all freshwater fishes.

Perhaps more than any other factor, successful trout fishermen realize the value of "matching the hatch" or knowing exactly what specific insects the trout in any given stream are eating and the circumstances surrounding their choices. To the casual observer, this might seem an easy task, but the truth is much advanced preparation, focus, and attention to detail is required for success. Although it's true that virtually all trout anglers are exposed to fly-casting techniques germane to the sport and carry a generic assortment of flies common to successful angling, savvy fishermen go beyond these areas.

In their quests to be the best, these elite anglers focus on details often overlooked by the majority of fishermen. For example, while average anglers stumble over rocky shorelines, bank on the knowledge of others, and pay little heed to the pools and eddies hiding their wary targets, upper echelon fishermen take the time to absorb the nuances of their immediate environment. They realize that overturning streamside rocks to ascertain exactly what insects recently hatched is a far better method than blindly casting a fly resembling bait that proved successful elsewhere.

They also understand the power of observation. Elite anglers are constantly noticing subtle nuances to the depth and flow of the stream, and seek out ambush areas where predators lie in wait for their prey. In addition, they note factors such as the direction and velocity of the wind, existing temperatures, and the emerging weather. In essence, successful anglers do the things that unsuccessful anglers don't and thus are rewarded for their efforts.

Anglers who are aware of their streamside environment notice things that others don't. In particular, they are aware of their own impact on the stream. For example, experienced fly fishermen know that casting their shadows across the stream can be a costly error. Instead, they make every attempt to blend in with their local environment.

Similarly, school stakeholders need to have a self-awareness to know what types of shadows they are casting and in what light other people are seeing them. They must acknowledge the tone and tenor of their relationships within the local school and community.

Trout anglers also realize that advanced preparation and the proper equipment are necessary for a successful trip. They arrive at the stream with an ample supply of time-tested flies and tackle. Similarly, savvy school change agents approach the campus with a working knowledge of strategies that are used elsewhere. This means they have absorbed information about how other schools across the country have handled situations similar to their own. Just like the angler knows that no two streams are alike, school stakeholders know that no two campuses are the same.

Armed with the right equipment, avid anglers absorb details from the surrounding environment. They hang out at the bait shop and talk to local experts. They chat about the best locations, current weather conditions, migration patterns, and levels of flow in the stream. Likewise, individuals interested in improving school safety ask the locals for their take on what's going on. They connect with local businesses, churches, and community organizations, speak with people who live there, and become part of the community. In essence, they find out what's going on from any and all sources.

The proper tools, knowledge, and information are necessary for a person to become an average fisherman. However, one factor separates the extraordinary fishermen from their peers—matching the hatch.

The way top-flight anglers do this is to take the time to unearth the direct food source at the stream. They literally turn rocks over at the streamside to look for the newly hatched insects that the trout are feeding on. Armed with this information, they are able to select precisely the right presentation. Often this involves creating an entirely new fly dedicated exclusively to a particular local stream.

Similarly, school stakeholders have an arsenal of proven strategies that have worked in other schools. In all likelihood, using these strategies will provide them with some level of success. Like trout fishermen who "match the hatch," superlative school leaders not only understand proven strategies, but also go the extra mile by tailoring their needs to their local campuses.

In essence, school stakeholders "match the hatch" by looking under every "rock" to find out who is involved in what situation and identify where, when, and why bullying is occurring on their campuses. They identify hot spots where students may be unsupervised. They monitor both schedules and time frames of bullying incidents. They take the time to speak with both bullies and victims in order to understand why bullying is occurring. Locally tailored intervention (matching the hatch) is the key to reducing bullying in your school.

Like the trout fishermen who do their advance work before arriving at the stream, school stakeholders who are confronted with bullying map their areas of focus in advance. Let's be clear, there are many school stakeholders who share concerns about improving both school safety and reducing levels of bullying. These include parents, community members, business owners, teachers, principals, and, perhaps most important, students themselves.

We dedicate this book to this diverse audience of individuals who are interested in "matching the hatch" in order to help create safe and bullying-free schools. In the following chapters, we present the "rocks" that you can overturn to begin matching your hatch.

In chapter 1, you will read about bullying as a growing problem in schools. The overview contained in the chapter begins with a clear definition of bullying. You will then look at the background of bullying, including some very large national and international studies to help you understand the probability of bullying occurring in your school. Next, you will view the tragic effects of bullying by profiling a number of incidents resulting in school violence. At the end of this chapter, you will have a good understanding of the broad scope of bullying occurring across the globe. You'll find that bullying is not an isolated phenomenon, and if your school or community is plagued by such incidents, you'll quickly realize you're not alone.

Chapter 2 presents the anatomy of a bully. One size doesn't fit all. This chapter outlines the misconceptions and ambiguities associated with profiling bullies and identifying bullying behaviors. Many may feel they know a bully's identity, but in this chapter, you'll see that bullies come in all shapes and sizes. You will look at the ways that the media portray bullying and how the prototype image of a bully put forth can be misconstrued and misunderstood. In this chapter, you will see how bullying presents itself differently from one community to another and also explore the intersection of the legal system as both a help and a hindrance to bully mitigation efforts.

Next, in chapter 3, we examine the effects that bullying among adults has on students. Students learn by observation. If they see adults in positions of power bullying their subordinates, they are likely to do the same, especially when they find themselves in positions of dominance. People in positions of power within a school have the potential to either help or hinder school safety efforts. Savvy school leaders not only espouse safe schools, they also model respectful behaviors to their subordinates. In addition, we present a number of important social factors that directly impact school safety. Through an examination of these variables, school stakeholders are exposed to specific strategies that they can use to reduce bullying on their campuses.

Chapter 4 examines bullying from the perpetrator's perspective. You will be presented with both the causes and the effects of bullying from the point of view of the bully and answer a variety of common questions, including the following: Why do individuals become bullies? How do they pick their targets? What motivates them to stop bullying? What advice would they give to school leaders who want to reduce bullying? This chapter also presents the possible long-term negative effects of bullying behaviors on the bullies themselves. Finally, chapter 4 includes an interview with a former bully, which exposes our readers to an insider's view of a very complex problem.

Contrasting the information from the previous section, chapter 5 examines bullying from the student victim's perspective. Here, you will read about the social interactions and relationships that are commonly noted by victims of bullying. There are both current and future challenges that victims of bullying encounter. This chapter identifies strategies our readers can use to help address these issues. Through specific media examples, you will see that anybody can be the victim of bullying.

In addition to bullies and victims, bystanders often witness these events. Chapter 6 investigates the concept of social proof, or the tendency of bystanders to look to their peers for socially acceptable behaviors. Important questions like these are addressed: Why are bystanders often passive when given opportunities to intervene? What motivates bystanders to get involved? To answer these questions, several research-based strategies are presented, which are designed to encourage bystanders to safely "get involved." Chapter 6 also includes current technologies available to both schools and communities that are dedicated to the reporting of bullying incidents.

Parents have an important role to play in the bullying cycle. Chapter 7 presents information on the impact of home environments on students' likelihood of becoming bullies, victims, or both. This chapter includes information on what parents can do to reduce the chances of their children being involved in bullying as well as the potential negative effects of helicopter parents, who are overly involved in their children's lives. You will also read about non-involved parents and the possible impacts that various parenting styles have on the likelihood of bullying.

Through the material presented in this chapter, you'll explore both proactive strategies and potential responses to bullying. In addition, you'll connect with the conundrum that many parents face when their child is first bullied. Questions like these are addressed: What are school protocols? Which school officials do I access when I learn of my child's involvement in bullying? How do I deescalate rather than escalate the situation in defense of my child? We discuss how to cope when policy compliance conflicts with the passion of protection. The material presented in chapter 7 brings to light possible strategies that parents can use to both protect their children and contribute to safe and healthy learning environments.

Families live in communities, and each local area has different norms for social interactions. Chapter 8 examines the relationships between bullying and community factors. Here you will explore cultural norms in the context of both overt (physical) and covert forms of bullying through the lens of cultural norms. In essence, we discuss the social standards of the community and how what is tolerated "on the street" may influence local perceptions of bullying. Also considered is the increasingly important role of the legal system in combating bullying incidents through formal interventions such as police, counseling, and social agencies. The chapter concludes by acknowledging how schools, religious institutions, community organizations, and families can provide exceptional sources of support if "street" norms conflict with socially accepted expectations.

Communities are no longer solely defined by geography. In the digital age, social communities have no boundaries. In chapter 9, the unique challenges of cyberbullying are presented along with an examination as to how the growing presence of social media affects online harassment. Examples of both children and their parents engaging in abusive online rhetoric are noted. The chapter also presents anecdotes in which schools have countered bullying by engaging in informed discussions with both parents and students to establish successful and safe online activities. This chapter concludes by discussing several online technologies designed to encourage the reporting of cyberbullying incidents.

We conclude our book by offering a user-friendly overview of research-based strategies designed for addressing the problem of bullying. Our strategies also include recommendations for superintendents, principals, teachers, parents, and students who are interested in bullying reduction efforts. To supplement our recommendations, we gift the Bully Index and a "hot spot" map to our readers so that schools can assess where and to what extent incidents of bullying are occurring on their campuses.

Chapter One

Bullying

A Substantial and Growing Problem

"The best indicator of a sociopathic serial bully is not a clinical diagnosis but the trail of devastation and destruction of lives and livelihoods surrounding this individual throughout their life."

—Tim Field, British anti-bullying activist

"Facts do not cease to exist because they are ignored."

—Aldous Huxley, author of *Brave New World*

Discussing bullying is closeted and largely remains a taboo subject, particularly for people directly involved or affected by it. Given both social and legal complexities associated with the act, bullies, victims, and/or school officials are reluctant to engage in extended conversations about bullying. For markedly different but obvious reasons, these constituencies generally seek to keep bullying to themselves. Most assuredly, student bullies have an obvious reason to keep the conversation quiet. It allows them to continue to operate without significant scrutiny.

Likewise, students who are bullied are just as likely to cloister their comments out of a desire to not be seen as a victim, or to avoid public embarrassment or shame. School officials can be the most reluctant of all groups to be transparent about bullying for fear of negative publicity. Indeed, many school officials worry that if questions are asked and discussions about bullying occur, parents will conclude that the school is unsafe. Thus, school stakeholders often assume an "ostrich mentality" when confronted with the issue by "burying their institutional heads in the sand" and resorting to a passive approach to addressing bullying. To be sure, many campus environments are characterized by a "just let sleeping dogs lie" philosophy.

As a result of student bullying in many schools being relegated to an un-mentionable topic, further institutional problems may surface, including more bullying incidents. Put simply, if students on campuses feel ashamed to admit they have been bullied, and if school leaders are burying the issue because they are worried about negative publicity, how can we know the true extent of bullying in schools?

For years, this dilemma has frustrated those interested in bullying reduction efforts. In fact, until the 1980s, there was almost no reliable data on the extent of bullying in schools. However, in 1982 a tragedy in Europe prompted change. In that year, three children in Bergen, Norway (ages 10–14), committed suicide. When it came to light that these children had all been victims of bullying, an outcry from the community to address this issue surfaced. As a result, public funding was allocated to assess the extent of the problem.

Researcher Daniel Olweus, a social science professor who had previously conducted smaller bullying studies, was targeted to lead this effort. The results of Olweus's research in Norway provided the first comprehensive examination of bullying in schools. For the purposes of benchmarking, we present a brief summary of Olweus's findings here.

- **Bullying prevalence rates:** 31.8 percent of students in grades 5–9 reported that they had been bullied at some point during the school year.
- **Bullying differences by gender:** The results of the research were slightly different from males to females, with 34 percent of boys indicating they had been the victims of bullying as compared with 29.5 percent of girls.[1]
- **Dual roles—bully and victim:** Olweus also found an important overlap between bullies and victims of bullies, with 20 percent of students who indicated involvement in bullying reporting that they had been both the victim of bullying and had also bullied other students.[2]
- **Frequency and duration:** Olweus also considered the frequency of bully-ing by categorizing responses according to: students who were not bullied at all, students who reported being bullied only once or twice during the school year, students who were bullied two to three times a month, and students who were subjected to bullying once a week or more.

By categorizing responses in this manner, Olweus assists in defining bul-lying by both frequency and duration. A student who has been the victim of verbal or physical aggression once might be categorized differently than someone who is repeatedly subjected to such attacks. Most researchers now define bullying as a negative act that occurs repeatedly over a period of time. Since Olweus's seminal investigation, numerous studies affirmed his original data. In sum, almost all bullying research shows that between 20–30 percent of students in grades 6 through 10 are involved in bullying either as bullies, victims, or both.[3]

WHEN DOES UNWANTED BEHAVIOR RISE TO THE LEVEL OF BULLYING?

There's no clear consensus on when unwanted behavior constitutes bullying. Complicating the issue is the fact that many researchers define bullying in different ways. This poses a serious problem for schools wishing to establish concise anti-bullying programs. Put simply, if there is no clear definition of what constitutes bullying, it is difficult (or nearly impossible) to combat the problem. When bullying is ill defined in an organization, multiple interpretations surface and ambiguity thwarts attempts to curb the behavior. In such schools, one person may construe a situation as "kids being kids," where another sees the incident as harassment.

BULLYING DEFINED

For the purposes of this book, we feel the U.S. Department of Health and Human Services offers a definition of bullying that encompasses many of the characteristics found in most descriptions of the act. As cited in the U.S. Department of Health and Human Services literature, "bullying is unwanted, aggressive behavior among school aged children that involves a real or perceived power imbalance. The behavior is repeated, or has the potential to be repeated, over time."[4]

Furthermore, in order to be considered bullying, the behavior must be aggressive and include the following:

- *A power differential:* People who bully use power to accomplish the task. Whether the source of power is physical strength, access to embarrassing information, verbal criticism, or greater popularity among their classmates, bullies use some source of power differential to control and intimidate their victims. Common bullying actions include making threats, spreading rumors, destroying property of the targeted person, attacking someone physically or verbally, intentionally excluding someone from a group, and generally forcing the victim to do something he/she does not want to do. Indeed, power differentials can shift over time and contexts such that one individual may be in a powerful position in one situation, but placed in a subordinate position when juxtaposed in a different social group.

• *Repetition:* Bullying usually involves behaviors that occur on more than one occasion.

The National Center for Education Statistics has compiled data from schools across the United States that indicates what specific types of bullying students are reporting. Although the data isn't surprising when compared to the prevailing research, a brief visual of the facts draws us to the conclusion that bullying continues to be both a pervasive and serious problem.

As figure 1.1 shows, bullying can take many different forms. Notwithstanding that 21.5 percent of all students responding to the NCES claim to be bullied at school, it's important for school and community stakeholders interested in addressing bullying to precisely distinguish what's occurring on campus. The largest group of students who are bullied report being made fun of, called names, or insulted (13.6 percent).

The second most common form of bullying is being the subject of rumors (13.2 percent). Interestingly, the data show the two most common forms of bullying are non-physical. Most folks may have thought of bullying as it relates to physical manifestations characterized by pushing, shoving, and hit-

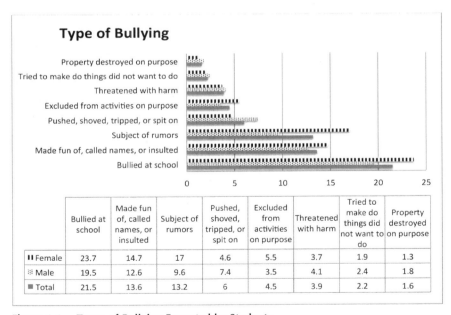

	Bullied at school	Made fun of, called names, or insulted	Subject of rumors	Pushed, shoved, tripped, or spit on	Excluded from activities on purpose	Threatened with harm	Tried to make do things did not want to do	Property destroyed on purpose
Female	23.7	14.7	17	4.6	5.5	3.7	1.9	1.3
Male	19.5	12.6	9.6	7.4	3.5	4.1	2.4	1.8
Total	21.5	13.6	13.2	6	4.5	3.9	2.2	1.6

Figure 1.1.   Types of Bullying Reported by Students
Source: National Center for Education Statistics. (2013). Percentage of students ages 12–18 who reported being bullied at school during the school year, by type of bullying and sex. Retrieved from https://nces.ed.gov/programs/digest/d14/tables/dt14_230.40.asp

ting. This is far from the truth. It is also interesting that females more often experience non-physical forms of bullying than males. However, this trend reverses for the third most reported form of bullying—where more boys than girls report they have been pushed, shoved, tripped, or spit on. Thus, boys appear to report higher levels of physical violence/physical threat than girls, while girls experience more bullying overall than boys (23.7 percent of girls compared to 19.5 percent of boys). Regardless of whether bullying is physical or psychological, it isn't gender specific and often causes serious harm to victims.[5]

Far less evident—but just as important—is the fact that the NCES data also confirm bullying in the United States exists at approximately the same level as it does internationally (21.5 percent of U.S. students report being bullied as compared with 31.8 percent in the Olweus study). Hence, bullying remains a global issue and represents a sociocultural problem that is certainly not confined to the United States.

THE LINK BETWEEN BULLYING AND SCHOOL VIOLENCE

Jefferson County, Colorado, is known as "The Gateway to the Rocky Mountains." The county seat is the city of Golden. In this pristine area of virgin forests, snow-capped mountains and natural springs abound. For people rooted there, Jefferson County represents the ideal place to raise a family, not the location of the deadliest high school shooting in United States history.

Tragically, millions of people watched live television feeds as students were ushered away from Columbine High School and police attempted to restore order on the campus. Subsequently, as details emerged, the facts pointed to a horrific realization: The shooters were actually Columbine students. Within minutes of the incident, puzzled observers asked, "How could this happen?" Following the incident, investigators concluded that students Eric Harris and Dylan Klebold, the shooters at Columbine High School, were victims of bullying before they became bullies themselves.

To substantiate this potentially lethal cycle of the bullied becoming the bully, a spattering of the testimonies taken from students close to the two Columbine assailants graphically illustrates a consistent pattern of bullying toward both Harris and Klebold. Alisa Owen was Harris's eighth-grade lab partner. According to her, Harris and Klebold were commonly bullied.[6]

Nathan Vanderau (a friend of Klebold) saw the same thing, noting that the worst incident he witnessed was when fellow students threw fecal matter at both Harris and Klebold.[7] Chad Laughlin was also a student at Columbine

High School. Though he was not a friend of Harris or Klebold, he remembers seeing them being picked on in the school cafeteria, the worst incident coming when upper classmen threw tampons that had been coated in ketchup at both Harris and Klebold.

To be sure, being bullied is not an excuse for violence. And after the tragic events that occurred at Columbine High School, many Americans began to ponder possible links between bullying and school violence. In fact, public awareness brought to light by the incident at Columbine prompted the U.S. Secret Service to conduct its own analysis of links between bullying and campus violence. Subsequently, Secret Service personnel examined all of the school shootings that occurred in the United States (37 total incidents) over a period of one year in order to determine whether previous incidences of bullying had significant impacts on the events. The results of the investigation pointed to the fact that bullying played a major role in two-thirds of these school shootings.[8]

To assume that every student who is bullied will become an active shooter is incorrect. In fact, out of the 50 million students enrolled in kindergarten through grade 12 in the United States, approximately 21.5 percent or 10.5 million students are bullied each year and 99.99 percent of them have not become active shooters. Thus, the prevailing Secret Service report represents a rather "double-edged sword" analysis, whereby it is much more accurate to state that the majority of school shootings in the United States are indeed perpetrated by individuals who have been bullied, but the vast majority of bullying victims do not commit acts of school violence.

THE LINK BETWEEN SCHOOL BULLYING AND SUICIDE

One of the most tragic results of bullying is that sometimes victims see suicide as their best option for escape. The Centers for Disease Control (CDC) reports that suicide is the third leading cause of death among young people with approximately 7 percent of high school students in the United States having attempted it. In addition, over 14 percent of the same group have considered suicide as an option for dealing with their life circumstances. Tragically, an average of 4,400 school-aged children commit suicide each year in the United States.[9] According to a review of suicide risk conducted by professors at Yale University, victims of bullying are two to nine times more likely to consider suicide than non-bullied individuals.[10] Similar studies indicate that approximately half of suicides among young people are related to bullying.[11]

There is no single criterion that makes an individual a likely candidate for ridicule from their peers. Anyone can be bullied. Consider 16-year-old Sladjana Vidovic. Her family had emigrated from Croatia to the small town of Mentor, Ohio. Voted by CNN and *Money Magazine* as one of the 100 best places to live, the Vidovic family thought they had picked the ideal spot to live out their American dream. That dream turned into a nightmare when their daughter committed suicide after unrelenting taunts from her high school classmates. What made this 16-year-old immigrant the source of ridicule was her Croatian accent, and an uncommon name, which her classmates intentionally mispronounced as "Slut–Jana." Although there was no evidence of promiscuity, Sladjana was routinely referred to as a slut. Tragically, this 16-year-old girl saw suicide as the best option to escape her tormentors.

Thankfully, not every student who is bullied will commit suicide. Tragically, far too many do. Therefore, careful vigilance on the part of parents and school stakeholders coupled with laws to protect students at home and in the classroom from psychological threats are warranted. As the story of Sladjana tragically illustrates, bullying victims are far more likely than non-bullying victims to attempt to end their own lives.[12]

THE LINK BETWEEN SCHOOL BULLYING AND REDUCED STUDENT LEARNING

Psychologists have discovered that individuals have certain needs that must be met before they can focus on learning endeavors. In fact, when people are worried about their safety, learning becomes difficult, if not impossible. Psychologist Abraham Maslow refers to specific life "priorities" as a hierarchy of needs. Take a look at figure 1.2, which illustrates Maslow's theory converted to a school context. In essence, the diagram focuses on the critical needs for a healthy student experience at school. As presented, the diagram consists of five specific ascending levels necessary for legitimate student development, with the primary concern of students being level 1—*survival needs* such as air, shelter, food, water, and sleep. Quite obviously, level 1 needs are paramount to existence, but what about level 2—*safety needs* such as protection from physical or verbal attacks? Employing the diagram, where would you put students who are being bullied at school? Imagine what being bullied does to students' abilities to advance their educational efforts to the next (or future) levels. In essence, if students are preoccupied with issues threatening their physical and emotional stability, socialization, self-esteem, and self-actualized needs will be neglected.

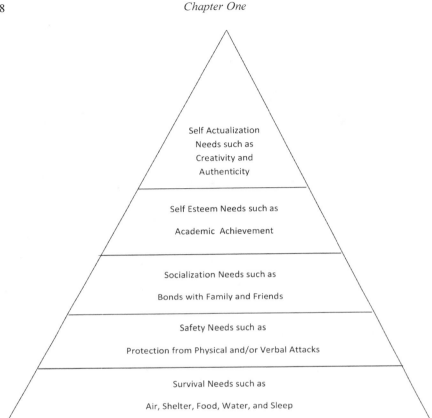

Figure 1.2. Adaptation of Maslow's Hierarchy of Needs to School Settings
Source: Maslow, A. H. (1954). *Motivation and personality.* New York, NY: Harper.

In truth, when confronted with bullies, many school-aged children choose to avoid school altogether. Hence, victims of bullying evidence higher rates of school avoidance and do not perform as well academically as their non-bullied peers.[13] Put simply, opportunities for these students to learn are limited by others, and they remain preoccupied by level 2 (*safety needs*).

According to the National Education Association, approximately 160,000 students stay home from school every day out of fear of being bullied.[14] Indeed, a growing group of students are facing level 2 (*safety*) challenges and are unable to focus beyond their immediate concerns. Seen in this context, the choice to avoid an unsafe situation by skipping school is understandable. Until these safety concerns are addressed, it seems fruitless to expect students to focus on academic achievements or engage in creative thinking. Quite frankly, it's no surprise researchers have found that students who are exposed to bullying are less engaged in their school work and have lower academic success than students who are not bullied.[15]

IMPACT OF SCHOOL BULLYING ON BOTH
THE BULLY AND HIS/HER VICTIM(S) OVER TIME

The impact of school bullying is felt far beyond school-aged years. Sociologists examining the long-term effects of bullying have found that both bullies and their victims experience negative influences well into adulthood.[16] For example, individuals who were bullied as children oftentimes continue to struggle with anxiety disorders as adults.[17] In fact, in many cases, anxiety is a learned response that these individuals employ when they encounter situations similar to those that resulted in bullying when they were younger.

Perhaps more surprising than the emotional and psychological consequences derived from being a victim of bullying is that bullies also experience negative effects of their actions well into adulthood. Specifically, former bullies have difficulty maintaining social relationships and report higher levels of loneliness and depression than the general population.[18] In many ways, bullies often become the victims of their own behaviors.

Facts

The consequences of bullying are both numerous and substantial. They include the potential for school violence, increased risk of suicide, and reduced student learning. Each day, as many as 160,000 students skip school in order to avoid the possibility of being bullied. Both bullies and their victims experience the effects of bullying well into adulthood.

Feelings

Emotions run high when it comes to bullying. These feelings can include anger, fear, resentment, anxiety, and depression. The students involved at the campus and the adults who care for them feel such emotions. Because of these strong feelings, there is a need for clear policies and procedures to address incidents of bullying. Bullies, bully victims, and even school leaders can be reluctant to talk about bullying. People interested in engaging these constituents in conversations about bullying need to be prepared to overcome this initial hurdle. School officials need to be aware of their own feelings when meting out punishment. It can be easy to forget that many students who bully were once bullied themselves. Implementing policies with fairness and kindness to all parties can substantially increase school safety.

Facilitation

All school and community constituents need to have a clear understanding of what constitutes bullying. It's the purview of school board members to establish the policies that define and provide consequences for various types of school bullying. It's the role of school administrators to administer those policies with fidelity, and it's the responsibility of classroom teachers to be on the lookout for bullying in all its varied forms.

NOTES

1. Solberg and Olweus (2003).
2. Solberg and Olweus (2003).
3. Nansel, Overpeck, Pilla, Raun, Simons-Morton, and Scheidt (2001).
4. United States Department of Health and Human Services (2016).
5. National Center for Education Statistics (2013).
6. Hill and Kurtis (2008).
7. Hill and Kurtis (2008).
8. Boodman (2006).
9. Centers for Disease Control and Prevention (2014).
10. Kim and Leventhal (2008).
11. Dickinson (2010).
12. Barr (2010).
13. Hanish and Guerra (2002); Rueger, Malecki, and Demaray (2011).
14. Van Roeckel (2012).
15. Cooper (2011); Nakamoto and Schwartz (2010); Rueger et al. (2011).
16. Kochenderfer-Ladd and Wardop (2001).
17. Hodges, Boivin, Vitaro, and Bukowski (1999).
18. Seals (2003).

Chapter Two

Anatomy of a Bully

One Size Doesn't Fit All

"'I have said a prayer to God,' wrote young Steven Shepherd, 'Why do I have to live like this? If I do I must kill myself.' He was a kid taunted as 'uneven Steven' because he walked with a limp resulting from a bus accident. In a stereotypical role, he wore thick glasses and nearly was blind if they were knocked off. He was roughed up hundreds of times and never learned to fight back. One day he just walked off 10 miles from town, tossing his glasses aside along the way, and he lay down in a ditch and eventually died there in a strawberry field, where he earlier had spent one truly happy day."[1]

We live in a world of the "Two C's." Indeed, convenience and consumption drive many decisions of both buyers and sellers. With millions of consumers seeking the latest and greatest products, corporate marketers often bombard shoppers with a "one size fits all" approach in order to maximize production and accommodate the ever-changing preferences of customers. To be sure, T-shirts, bracelets, hats, socks, gloves, sunglasses, watch bands, ties, and even ponchos are now identified as "one size fits all" to group consumers into more profitable market categories for businesses. Put simply, it's pretty convenient for businesses to lump a large group of consumers together into a standard profile and then deal with them by offering a uniform product.

Unfortunately, simple business processes like identifying the right mix of people, determining their buying tendencies, and categorizing them into one large cluster of behavior doesn't extend to bullies and their characteristics. In other words, when it comes to bullies, the "one size fits all" characterization simply doesn't apply. In fact, although much is known about bullies and their general physical, social, and environmental attributes, it's pretty misleading to assume that we can predict what a "typical bully" will look like. That said, school stakeholders who identify bullies by noting "traditional" characteristics address a large portion of the problem and that's an important first step in establishing a bully-free campus. However, identifying bullies and curbing their behaviors are separate issues. Thus, a good, old-fashioned look at what's known about bullies and how this information can be both a blessing and a challenge for school leaders is definitely in order.

BULLYING: WHAT WE KNOW

The most common link between all bullying incidents is that they almost always involve three groups: bullies, victims, and bystanders. The bullying research points to one certainty: bullies need to feel powerful and in control. In addition, oftentimes they derive satisfaction from inflicting injury and suffering on others, have limited empathy for their victims, and defend their actions by saying that their victims provoked them in some way.

Besides their cravings to feel powerful and controlling, bullies are provocative and much more aggressive individuals than most students. But that behavioral mix doesn't mean that profiling is the solution to this problem. To date, there's no clinical typecast of a bully, nor is there any consistent way to classify people into one of the three categories.[2] The roles of bully, victim, and bystander aren't fixed, and some students alternate between them. In cases where kids jump between bully and victim, each respective identity surfaces at different times and can certainly cloud the issue of identification. That's where sorting out the details of bullying gets tough for school stakeholders.

Although typical media portrayals of bullies stereotype them as huge, hulking punishers with hair-trigger sensitivities, the truth is that people who bully possess few clear-cut characteristics other than they are generally stronger than their victims and actively seek to dominate them either physically or psychologically. These types of children are commonly referred to as "aggressive" bullies and are relatively easy to pinpoint. Once identified by deed or action, it then becomes a matter of interviewing, confirming, and reprimanding them.

Aggressive bullies tend to be overt personalities, belligerent, fearless, coercive, confident, tough, and impulsive. Their actions are more direct and physical; these include hitting, poking, tripping, slapping, name calling, making racist remarks, and constant teasing. This type of behavior typically comes from a bully who has a low tolerance for frustration and a reliance on violence. Aggressive bullies are more defiant or oppositional toward adults, tend to be antisocial, and are apt to challenge school rules. In sum, school bullies who fit into the aggressive "bigger and stronger" areas are the easiest to identify and control.

It's a bit more challenging to target "passive" bullies who operate clandestinely in the schoolyard shadows or via cyberspace. Passive bullies (sometimes referred to as relational bullies) rarely provoke others or take the physical initiative in a bullying incident. Their actions are usually indirect and more emotional or passive-aggressive, and involve acts characterized by social isolation or manipulation to harm another. This type of personality sometimes aligns with more powerful perpetrators and elevates their participation once the overt bullying begins.[3] In essence, passive bullies often "pile on" previously identified victims and use more covert methods of abuse than aggressive bullies employ.

Being a bully doesn't necessarily require Herculean strength or a high IQ. Getting right down to it, the real challenge for school leaders seeking to eliminate bullying on their campuses is to *confront and control both active aggressive and passive bullies*. Much of the existing research on bullies identifies their problems as being pathological in nature and oftentimes indicative of psychiatric disorders.[4]

In general, bullying often relates to pathogical beginnings anchored in such areas as the child's family, school, or local community. A closer look at the potential connection of each of these areas provides school personnel with important information that is useful to understanding the constitution of a bully.

BULLYING AND FAMILY BACKGROUND

Bullies often come from problem families where parental rejection or abuse is the rule. Children and adolescents who bully may have been victims of both domestic violence and abuse.[5] It's also not uncommon for bullies to witness their parents abusing other family members.

The parents of bullies tend to use harsh discipline, combined with physical punishment and violence, as a way to resolve family problems.[6] In short, the old adage that "people do what people see" rings very true when applied to children who bully. In essence, "bullies at school are often victims at home."[7] Without question, young people who are exposed to a steady diet of family violence often respond as school bullies.

BULLYING AND SCHOOL

A school's social norms also can undeniably influence bullies. The daily interaction of students with the school environment legitimates established social norms, which surface as either positive or negative. Thus, antisocial peer interactions within the school directly influence bullying or victimization. For example, if a student's peer group tolerates or encourages bullying, then the student is more likely to participate in these behaviors.[8] Likewise, teachers may also unintentionally facilitate bullying by haphazardly monitoring students during unstructured times such as recess or bus duty. By failing to directly and immediately act in response to reports of bullying, bullies process the actions as legitimate and beneficial to their positions.[9] Under these circumstances, welcome to trouble with a capital T.

BULLYING AND THE COMMUNITY

A child's propensity to bully is also influenced by the local community. When a student's family, peers, and school exist within the boundaries of a community known for elevated levels of violence, aggression is both perpetuated and condoned. In other words, bullies feel at home in areas where both violence and aggression are accepted. In such neighborhoods, dominance and intimidation are prized, and the cultural norms and beliefs of the student's community reinforce the acceptance of bullies as regular parts of the social landscape.[10] There again, in communities where "mean streets" exist, schools are charged to deal with a "two-headed monster." On the one hand, they must ensure that all students have opportunities to learn in bully-free campus environments. Additionally, they must engage in social processes that extend that mind-set to the neighborhood populations.

Although changing community norms may seem like a daunting task for teachers and administrators, rest assured it is achievable. Through careful planning in collaboration with community members to create anti-bullying policies, schools stand a far greater chance of creating meaningful change than if they were to operate in isolation. When it comes to bullying, the community is watching.

When an incident of bullying occurs, the way the school responds will speak volumes about what is acceptable in the community and what is not, particularly when those norms are reinforced by local stakeholders. At this juncture, it's important to remember that *for members of the school community, the most important issues are to curb, control, and eliminate campus bullying and then deal with the psychological "baggage" of the perpetrator.*

One caveat is in order. As a general rule, deal with the immediate problem of controlling bullying *unless* the psychological "baggage" of the bully jeopardizes school safety. In such cases, school officials, in concert with available legal resources, must intervene to protect all stakeholders. In a nutshell, school administrators who proactively implement measures to stop bullying stand much better chances of gaining student, teacher, and community support for future interventions. By involving the school staff, students, families, and community members as active partners in the process, progress is within your reach. Advice? Be proactive rather than reactive and forge ahead by dedicating yourselves to your schools, stakeholders, and communities.

ROOTING OUT BULLIES BY IDENTIFYING THE VICTIMS

Since bullies can be difficult to spot, it might be easier to root out bullies by looking for their victims. In essence, this strategy is akin to the "tail wagging the dog," but whatever works is a legitimate course of action when it comes to stemming school bullying. To be sure, there are certain commonalities among victims of bullying. For example, people who are overweight tend to be bullied more than their peers. While 25 percent of boys and 33 percent of girls report having been teased about their weight, the number rises to 60 percent among overweight students.[11]

Individuals with disabilities are also at increased risk for victimization. According to the National Autistic Society, approximately 50 percent of children with autism or Asperger's syndrome have experienced bullying. Students also can be targeted for bullying based on their sexual orientations. The Gay, Lesbian, and Straight Education Network surveyed students from 2,770 school districts in all 50 states, and found that 55 percent of students who self-identify as lesbian, gay, bisexual, transgendered, or queer (LGBTQ) reported being verbally harassed, and 23 percent reported being physically hassled.

Just as one size doesn't fit all among bullies, the same is true of their victims. Anyone can be a victim of bullying. Students who are overweight, disabled, or identify as LGBTQ are not the only ones who experience bullying. Most definitely, power differentials also can be created by differences in popularity, social class, wealth, knowledge of potentially embarrassing information, or a number of other factors. Thus, even stars of both the football team and scholastic bowl can be victims of bullying.

One disturbing example of the murky nature of bullying serves as a testimony that not every situation is clear. In 2013, a 16-year-old male student died after being punched and pushed against a wall by a fellow student. During the court case, both sides acknowledged that the student who was killed had been teasing the assailant by throwing wadded up pieces of paper and erasers at him, and hitting him in the groin. The victim of the initial behavior

then became the aggressor, punching the other student twice, which ultimately resulted in the student's death.[12]

This tragic account is just one of many demonstrating that identities of
bullies and victims cannot only blur, but also reverse, with former victims
becoming perpetrators. While there are some groups that are more suceptible
to being bullied than others, given the right circumstances, anyone can be the
victim of bullying.

BULLYING: WHAT WE DON'T KNOW
AND WHAT WE CAN DO TO FIND OUT

When first encountered, most teachers and administrators are exposed to
fairly clear-cut examples of bullying. These "first blush" incidents deal in the
"no doubt" realm and easily slip into what's known about the classic bully/
victim exchange. To be honest, those are the easy fixes when it comes to
dealing with bullying. The going gets tougher when bullying is camouflaged
through various school personalities and factors.

Compounding the challenge of available knowledge and the linkage to
bullying is the fact that there's a lot researchers don't yet know about bullying. Although having access to existing bullying information is important in
providing guidance about the greatest risk factors, the fact is no amount of
national data can provide a full picture of specific bullying on your campus.
Thus, local information is essential.

Like an ostrich that buries its head in the sand hoping to avoid its enemy,
many school leaders hesitate to openly and honestly discuss bullying. Often
this apprehension is based on the fact that administrators just don't know
how to approach various constituencies within their schools about the topic.
If they begin to talk about curbing bullying on their campuses, will this scare
the community? Parents might ask, "Why is this school talking about bullying when others aren't? Does this mean that there is a bigger problem of
bullying on this campus than at schools that aren't talking about it?" These
are sobering considerations for school leaders, who are pressed by both public
perceptions and district mandates.

Likewise, if principals choose a more proactive approach and send surveys
home that ask parents or students about their perceptions of bullying, will
an anxious parent contact the local news to say, "Hey, look what my child's
campus sent home—they must have a bullying problem—go investigate."
Certainly, in this day and age, no school board or superintendent is going to
be pleased if a bullying story makes the local news. Sadly, the prospect of
raising media "red flags" drives many administrators to avoid having meaningful conversations about bullying . . . until it is too late.

In order to address bullying head on, understanding that bullies come in all shapes and sizes is critical. Bullies can be jocks, cheerleaders, nerds, band geeks, or any student walking down the halls. And students aren't the only ones who bully. As we will explore, bullies can also be teachers, administrators, or even parents.

Wherever there is a power differential, there is an opportunity for bullying. Put simply, many children look to the adults within their community to learn how they should act when they are in positions of power. If kids see adults abusing power differentials, they are more likely to do the same. Truly, there is much adults can do to reduce the likelihood of bullying. Those strategies are explored in a coming chapter.

Finally, initiating the fight against school bullying is relatively easy. It's winning that struggle that's the real challenge. Beginning the battle against bullying is much like steering an elephant. Seated atop Dumbo, we know what we want to happen, tell everyone where we're going, and how we're going to get there. But until the elephant starts moving, we aren't going anywhere. In other words, an elephant can't be steered until it's moving! Likewise, only after we've created momentum in the fight against bullies (which may take some encouraging prodding, enthusiastic poking, and the sheer will to succeed) is it possible for us to steer our bullying elephant.

Let's make something very clear. School officials who take proactive approaches to bullying by working with local stakeholders to identify when, where, and to what extent bullying is occurring on campus hold a huge advantage over those who don't. So . . . hop aboard that elephant on your campus, establish some movement in your journey to eliminate bullying—by understanding what we know and coming to grips with what we don't know about bullies—and steer your school to safety.

Facts

- Bullies come in all shapes and sizes. One size does not fit all.
- Bullying nearly always involves three parties: the bully, the victim, and bystanders.
- The roles of bully, victim, and bystander are not fixed, and some students alternate between them.

Feelings

Bullies have a need to feel powerful and in control, and are generally stronger or more powerful in some way than the people they target. Bullies seek to dominate their victims either physically or psychologically.

Facilitation

Most bullies are products of their environment. Though not always the case, bullies often come from problem families where parental rejection or abuse is common. Individuals looking to curb incidents of bullying should begin by looking for ways to strengthen home and family support structures.

Antisocial peer interactions within the school directly influence bullying and victimization. The peer pressure that is created can be positive or negative. When a group of "mean kids" get together, they can spur each other on to deeper and deeper levels of ridicule and hate. In order to address this problem, savvy administrators may consider working with informal student leaders who are looked up to by their peers to help establish positive peer interactions.

A child's propensity to bully is also influenced by the local community. As a member of the community, the most important step to take is to work with your local school to create a plan to curb and control existing risk factors that can lead to bullying. School officials who take proactive approaches by working with local stakeholders to identify when, where, and to what extent bullying is occurring on campus hold a huge advantage over those who don't.

NOTES

1. Elvin (2001, p. 48).
2. Bosworth, Espelage, and Simon (1999).
3. Schwartz et al. (2001).
4. Juvonen and Graham (2001).
5. U.S. Department of Health and Human Services (2001).
6. Hann and Borek (2002).
7. Batsche (1997, p. 172).
8. Swearer and Espelage (2004).
9. Craig, Pepler, and Atlas (2000).
10. Swearer and Espelage (2004).
11. Puhl, Luedicke, and Heuer (2011).
12. *San Antonio Express News* (2014).

Chapter Three

Bullying among
Adults within the Organization

"In school they call it bullying but at work they call it upper level management."

—Anonymous

"Workplace bullying—in any form—is bad for business. It destroys teamwork, commitment and morale."

—Tony Morgan, chief executive of the Industrial Society

"Bullying consists of the least competent most aggressive employee projecting their incompetence on to the least aggressive most competent employee and winning."

—Tim Fields, British anti-bullying activist

The University of Alabama's football team represents one of the most storied college programs in the history of the sport. The "Crimson Tide," which is the team's nickname, has amassed an impressive array of NCAA football records since the program's inception in 1892. The records of the team affectionately known by its fans as "Bama" span 124 seasons and include 864 total victories, 16 national championships, 30 conference titles, and 64 post-season bowl appearances resulting in 34 wins and two Heisman trophies (awarded to the nation's top college football player).

Often heralded as one of college football's greatest programs, expectations for success run high each season. Fans, faculty of the university, and coaches anticipate that the "Bama" football team will consistently perform at a championship level. Most recently, the University of Alabama was recognized as the 2015 Football Bowl Series (FBS) national champion after defeating Clemson University in the final game of the season.

Much of Alabama's recent football success is credited to current head coach Nick Sabin and his staff of experienced associates. Indeed, football pundits and sportscasters frequently tout Sabin's assistant coaches and his ability to organize them for much of the team's success. However, recently the college football world was stunned by the announcement on December 12, 2016, that third-year offensive coordinator Lane Kiffin had accepted a head coaching position at Florida Atlantic University, a school whose football reputation is little known compared to that of the University of Alabama.

Why would a highly successful coach who had guided the Alabama offense to three outstanding seasons and produced two Heisman Trophy winners leave such a position? Why would Lane Kiffin suffer a cut in his salary to assume the reins of a mediocre college football program?

While both sports news experts and fans pondered these questions, many football insiders pointed to the possibility of workplace bullying as the reason why Kiffin chose to leave.[1] In fact, it was widely speculated that the public berating of Kiffin by an angry Sabin during Alabama's second win of the 2016 season, a resounding 38–10 win over Western Kentucky University, proved to be the proverbial "tipping point."

With the outcome of the game in little doubt, Sabin became incensed over a play Kiffin had called that led to a miscue by the Alabama offense. In front of players, coaches, fans, and the national media, television cameras recorded Sabin viciously haranguing his assistant coach on the sidelines while stunned bystanders watched. When asked by a reporter at the post-game press conference about the "arguments" between him and Kiffin, Sabin replied, "There's no arguments. Those are called ass chewings."

The sport of football is an American pastime. Bullying is not. Although rarely caught on film, episodes such as the one that occurred between one of the nation's premier college football coaches and his top assistant are all too familiar. Bullying among adults is common both at home and in the workplace. And due to the absence of laws governing such behavior, it's flourishing.

NOW YOU SEE IT, AND NOW
YOU DON'T: THE LAW THAT ISN'T

Across the nation, scores of policies, local statutes, and state laws addressing bullying in schools exist. Although it's often difficult to enforce some of these regulations due to a perplexing array of legal interpretations and a lack of institutional understanding, laws against such behavior assist us in combating campus bullying. Regrettably, similar laws protecting adults from bullying, intimidation, and workplace hostility are nonexistent. In fact, although workplace bullying is four times more common than sexual harassment or racial discrimination, it isn't illegal.[2]

This poses a challenge for the school-age generation about to assume positions in the workplace. They've been taught that bullying is taboo and won't be tolerated. They've also been warned about participating in bullying, including both the penalties and ramifications resulting from such actions. Thanks to proactive school officials and their legislative counterparts, most students know their rights and responsibilities when it comes to bullying. However, without similar workplace legislation it's quite possible that future generations of workers will be unable to cope with these prevailing conditions.

In a sense, tomorrow's employees pipelining from our nation's schools into the workplace are in a "now you see it, and now you don't" situation. They have been exposed to civility through regulations, policies, and examples in their schools, but now see their training give way to a workplace environment that has little application of it. At best, this potential situation will prompt interruptions in the productive flow of businesses. At worst, the condition could require an additional bureaucratic "layer" designed to assist workers traumatized by hostile (bullying) environments. As a result, the by-products of workplace bullying produce diminished productivity and increased costs, two factors businesses can ill afford.

The sad news is that advocates supporting laws against workplace bullying have not been successful. As of 2017, only the state of Tennessee incorporates legislation that prohibits such behavior, but this applies only to government workers. In fact, one of the most viable pieces of anti-bullying legislation to be introduced, the Healthy Workplace Bill, has met with little success given that 28 states have failed to enact the statute and only one has passed it.

Due to the general sense of apathy toward both workplace bullying and stakeholder victimization, employees continue to pursue cautious approaches in regard to filing complaints over such matters with human resource departments. In absence of legal protections, the cost of reporting workplace bullying could jeopardize one's employment. In an attempt to abort the conditions of bullying at work, many employees are forced to use other "protected class" categories to combat the effects of the aggression.

Interventions by employees based on the National Labor Relations Act and discrimination claims based on race, sexual orientation, religion, gender, and national origin are often engaged as surrogates to replace nonexistent anti-bullying regulations in the workplace. Adult workplace bullying continues to hamper both individual and business performance and remains largely unchecked. The fact is that many little bullies become big ones . . . and the big ones are more sophisticated and oftentimes more difficult to detect.

TYPES OF ADULT BULLIES

Based on the dictates of modern society, it's a pretty standard expectation that as our lives progress, so do we. We leave childish behaviors behind in favor of mature adult interactions. But sometimes this just isn't the case. Some adults hold to the bullying behaviors of their youth and simply apply a greater degree of sophistication to the craft. While it's true that the majority of adult bullying is verbal, other methodologies are employed by bullies to accomplish their goals of dominance and power. Akin to their childhood habits, adult bullies want to show everyone in their social orbit "who's the boss," and several prototypes exist.

- *The Brute or Physical Bully:* Resting on the seldom employed "bottom rung" of the adult bullying type is the physical bully. Physicality is not the preferred tool of the adult bullying trade, but some resort to it. Unlike their youthful counterparts, the physical bully will usually not enter into a direct altercation with a victim, choosing instead to vandalize another person's property or steal their belongings to force the issue.

  Physical bullies generally threaten harm or invade the "space" of a victim rather than directly assaulting them. All told, physical bullies are rare in the adult world, but they do exist. If confronted by a physical bully, stay calm, exit the circumstances as soon as possible, never return the abuse, and as an adult realize there are consequences if you choose to play the victim.

- *The Spontaneous Bully:* The expression "heat of the moment" aptly characterizes the actions and responses of spontaneous adult bullies. As their name implies, spontaneous bullies have "short fuses" and give little heed to preplanning their victimization. It's interesting to note that spontaneous bullies are the most prone to formal discipline. Because they have a difficult time restraining their emotional reactions to immediate situations, they tend to create havoc at a moment's notice thereby incurring greater public scrutiny. That said, many spontaneous bullies "emit" unintentionally and lash out at their victims due to completely unrelated factors such as personal stress and previous mood-altering experiences that occurred outside the current incident.

- *The Egomaniac:* More deeply troubled than most other adult bullying types, narcissistic or ego-driven bullies are consumed with themselves.

They represent the archetype of both ego and selfishness, demonstrating a total disregard for others. They lack the ability to relate to people and exhibit very little apprehension about the outcomes of their victimization. Due to their fragile psychological nature, narcissistic bullies are in constant need of victims to belittle.

* *The Verbal Bully:* Ranking as one of the most sophisticated of the adult bullying types, verbal bullies use a number of strategies to cleverly avoid detection. Verbal bullies specialize in flying "under the radar" and accomplish much of their damage by humiliating others through sarcasm, subtle but vitriolic diatribes, and initiating falsehoods and rumors about their victims.

    Verbal types represent the largest identifiable adult bullying group. Their actions usually are hard to document. Verbal adult bullies pride themselves on their "Teflon" nature—that is, their abilities to cloud the circumstances of the victimization so nothing will "stick" to them. Needless to say, the effects of verbal bullying on victims can be extremely damaging both psychologically and emotionally.

Sadly, there's little that can be done about adult bullying. As we've seen, schools constitute environments that proactively engage anti-bullying through specific policies, clear-cut regulations, and proactive enforcement. On the other hand, the workplace represents an entirely different scenario where ignoring the problem (and relocating away from the bully) is often the only option once a supervisor has been notified of the behavior.

The fact is, adult bullies like what they're doing and are determined to maintain their status as purveyors of abuse. They're simply not interested in compromises or acting for the good of the order. Adults who bully are interested in dominating others and little else. However, whether the bully is an adult or a child, their message is always the same . . . power, intimidation, and abuse of those perceived as vulnerable.

THE SERIAL BULLY: SOCIOPATH AT WORK

By far, the serial bully is the most nefarious and can encompass a wide range of the bullying prototypes discussed earlier. Representing the bull in the organizational china shop, serial bullies seek positions of authority and foster false trust to improve their personal situations. In the process, they damage both the workplace environment and the people under their control. Still, serial bullies don't necessarily have to hold positions of authority in an organization, but they can be distinguished by their behaviors.

As the name implies, serial bullies are, in essence, addicted to predation and relish transitioning from bullying one victim to another.[3] They are ruthless in their pursuits but artfully conceal their actions behind power and authority in an attempt to appear civilized. Rarely using physical violence or verbal outbursts, the serial bully employs sophisticated, but subtle, techniques such as institutional authority, rumormongering, and discreet one-on-one abuse to achieve dominance over his or her prey. They're also extremely adept at deception and frequently camouflage their actions by using subordinates to accomplish their dirty work.

Serial bullies are classic manipulators. They are highly focused on accomplishing their goals, which are to establish credibility as an organizational leader while wreaking havoc on anyone they feel impedes their purpose. Serial bullies are value claimers. They extract much more from the organization than they contribute. Through complex psychological mixes of charm, flattery, false concern, and charisma, they painstakingly craft impressions of competence and care in order to cloak their personal intents. Serial bullies also are adept at impression building and will go to great lengths to convince others they are genuine, including concocting grandiose stories about their accomplishments, resorting to name-dropping, and parroting behaviors of others who have earned legitimacy in the organization.

Initially, many stakeholders will buy into the serial bully's game, but eventually his or her actions begin to change opinions. Through repeated examples of bullying, the word gets out, and although fear restricts some in the organization from recognizing the true nature of the serial bully, many come to realize that ruthlessness, aggression, deceit, and unmitigated selfishness are being employed to advance him or her at the expense of others. Indeed, individuals who expose the serial bully's true nature often become those most likely to be targeted.

When serial bullies feel threatened by competent and popular coworkers, they rally behind previously successful bullying techniques to discredit their opposition. In these situations, it's common for serial bullies to resort to heightened criticism, attacking a victim's integrity, and manufacturing outright falsehoods to try to divert scrutiny away from themselves. With total disregard for the organizational contributions of competent individuals, serial bullies develop a laser-like preoccupation with destroying the self-esteem and reputations of their victims. As they ratchet up their efforts, serial bullies combat defensive actions put forth by victims via intensifying their attempts to discredit them with administrators and colleagues. Ultimately, the initial bullying of the victim is now replaced by a more insidious and refined attempt to force them out of the environment through dismissal or resignation. If this occurs, the serial bully's actions are then refocused on his or her next organizational victim, and the sequence begins again.

Unfortunately, countless examples of such workplace behaviors exist. All too frequently, bullying "bosses" resort to abusive serial behaviors targeting competent subordinates by cloaking their addiction to mistreatment under the guise of exaggerated work schedules, belittling gossip, and accusations of illicit behaviors by the victim. With pinpoint accuracy honed through years of experience, serial bullies strategically stage events to appear that the victim merits the indictment. Sadly, serial bullies relentlessly dedicate their actions to securing the removal of victims whom they see as threats to their position in the organization.

RESPONDING TO ADULT BULLYING

From the adult bullying information presented thus far, some readers may find themselves discouraged. After all, with a growing number of adult bullies prowling the workplace in search of victims, the prospects of avoiding such situations seem slim. Is the adult workplace environment destined for habitual bullying? Definitely not! There are specific actions regarding what to do and what *not* to do that can help stakeholders both avoid the pitfalls of workplace bullying and diminish its effects if they do occur.

What to Do When Addressing Workplace Bullying

- *Decide that you will not be the victim.* A deliberate and conscious decision to stand up to a bully goes a long way toward successfully confronting the problem. Workplace bullies are usually not overt in their actions. Deciding to publicly expose them prompts attention they don't relish.
- *Confide in a trusted colleague.* Safe spaces thwart bullies and comfort those who are targeted by them. By locating a trusted colleague and sharing the specifics of what's occurring victims often find relief. Victims who clarify their positions with a colleague enlist a confidant who lends a sympathetic and objective voice to the issue.[4]
- *Recruit a witness to attest to the bullying.* Most bullies are creatures of habit. They operate at specific times and use certain places. In other words, bullies are predictable. If at all possible, arrange for a witness to be on hand when bullying is likely to occur. The credibility of someone who is bullied is exponentially enhanced when a witness supports the victim's story.[5]
- *Meticulously document the events.* Always document the details of a bullying incident. Minor details can produce major outcomes when it comes to reporting bullying so be vigilant and timely when recording information about the circumstances.

What Not to Do When Addressing Workplace Bullying

- *Don't reciprocate.* Resist the urge to "feed the beast" by fighting back against the bully. Victims who physically respond to adult bullying play directly into the aggressor's hands, particularly since the majority of workplace bullying is not physical. By resorting to any type of physicality in response to bullying, bystanders may well be confused about the actual source of the problem. The victim who resorts to a physical response to the bully may find him or herself explaining their actions to superiors. Rule one? Never start two fires trying to put one out.

- *Avoid becoming a bullying clone.* Author and leadership guru John Maxwell maintains that "hurting people hurt people."[6] It may come as a surprise, but some victims of adult bullying succumb to the frustration of the experience by becoming bullies themselves. Joining the "dark side" by becoming a bully will only compound a difficult situation, demean the victim's legitimacy in the organization, and exacerbate feelings of resentment and anger. Plus, the original perpetrator will shield his or her behaviors behind the newer bully's aggression!

- *Never contemplate the worst.* In extreme cases, victims of workplace bullying weigh more extreme solutions to their problems. Under no circumstances should victims consider harming themselves (or others) in an attempt to escape bullying. Regardless of the type, degree, intensity, or frequency of the victimization, there is always help at hand! If need be, victims should seek professional help to deal with the personal angst generated by being bullied through the use of the following agencies and resources:

  o If someone is in imminent danger, call 911.
  o If you are contemplating suicide, call 911 or the National Suicide Prevention Hotline: 1-800-273-TALK (8255).
  o For general resources on bullying, go to: www.stopbullying.gov.
  o For additional resources on workplace bullying, go to www.workplace bullying.org.
  o For help answering mental health insurance questions, go to:https://www .hhs.gov/mental-health-and-addiction-insurance-help.
  o *Most importantly, we recommend that individuals who are psychologically impacted by workplace bullying seek help from a local mental health provider.

- *Resist projecting your frustrations.* Many adult victims keep the bullying situation to themselves. They incorrectly assume that as an adult there is something wrong with reporting the bullying to formal entities such as management or human resources. These misguided assumptions lead to severely repressed layers of anger, which often emerge in daily contacts with both friends and family members. Loved ones and colleagues become confused and shaken when bullying victims launch assaults toward them with little or no provocation. For very obvious reasons, victims should never carry the weight of bullying with them.

ADULT BULLYING IN SCHOOLS: WHO'S WEARING THE "BIG BOY" PANTS?

Schools represent highly specialized workplaces. There is greater social sensitivity in a school than a typical workplace. For example, an isolated or inhibited child is much more likely to be targeted by bullies than an adult who wishes to be left alone to do their job, work their "straight eight," and go home. In fact, by necessity, the work environment enveloping schools is especially attuned to stakeholders communicating more personally and intimately than other workplaces. Thus, one of the major cultural attributes of the school environment is heightened sensitivity to positive or negative actions. Students often are keenly aware of social interactions taking place on campus and quickly discern both positive and negative nuances in relationships.

It's a fact that students are the most visible (and regulated) group on school campuses. Much time and effort is dedicated to imparting an awareness of existing rules and regulations to them, and for the most part, students adhere to these rules. But what happens when the kids aren't the problem and the adults at school are the bullies? In those circumstances, it's time to determine who's wearing the "big boy" pants.

Schools represent ideal social spaces for kids to watch adult relationships and learn how to interact with others in situations involving power differentials.[7] If students are exposed to healthy, open, and productive relations among teacher colleagues, support staff, and the administration, they absorb proper social instruction that paves the way for both successful and future workplace exchanges. For example, when students consistently see teachers exhibiting courtesy and respect to paraprofessionals, a message of organizational equity and equality is translated. Likewise, students observing campus administrators valuing faculty members in professional and appreciative ways recognize that cooperation is more effective than dominating subordinates through the power of a title.

Conversely, school workplaces burdened with adults preoccupied with positional power and abusing personal privileges also relay messages to students. In these environments, the lesson is that rank and power are tools to be used to leverage personal gain. In such schools, adults model workplace relations predicated on "lording it over others."

Teachers who openly disrespect campus service workers and publicly chastise classroom aides communicate that bullying and abusive behaviors are standards by which success is achieved. In addition, school administrators who regularly seize opportunities to demean the faculty encourage similar behaviors in students. Given their observances, students come to believe that bullying is a means to an end. They're socialized to think that—despite existing policies against bullying—power, force, and dominance are the keys to success. In short, students come to believe that civility simply doesn't matter.

Without question, workplace bullying by adults threatens productivity and saps organizational energy, but in schools, the outcomes of such behavior are especially detrimental. The stakes are extraordinarily high because students observe bullying behavior condoned by adults and often mold it into their future vocational experiences. That said, there's an even greater risk at hand . . . when students become the targets of school-based bullying by teachers.

THE TEACHER AS BULLY:
A WOLF IN SHEEP'S CLOTHING

When the subject of bullying in schools is discussed, most people think of student-on-student situations. However, bullies don't discriminate, and adults who bully in schools can and do prey on students. Yes, indeed, even teachers bully students! Under the guise of "doing what's best for the student," teachers, coaches, and other school personnel can and do resort to bullying. Some of the "professionals" to which parents entrust their children actually serve as educational "wolves in sheep's clothing" by claiming to act in the best interests of the students, while in reality preying on them. In order to grasp the issue of teachers bullying students, a bit of reflection about what previously was acceptable in schools versus what is currently deemed appropriate is in order.

In the past, permissible student disciplinary measures employed by teachers (and other school personnel) commonly included corporal actions such as paddling, slapping, grabbing, or pushing students. Teachers often engaged in the public humiliation of students via name calling, reporting poor grade performances to the entire class, drawing attention to dress or hygiene factors, and relocating "offenders" to the corners of a classroom, hallway, or athletic field. For the most part, these past practices are now deemed archaic. In addition, teachers still resorting to these actions are likely to be sanctioned, both publicly and by formal school policies. In response to such behaviors, legal action also is often taken against both the individual and the school district.

The insidious part of the teacher-bullying-student equation is that incidents often go unreported. In many cases, students are formally discouraged from reporting the abuse. After all, what school administrator wants to report that there are problems of teachers bullying students on his or her campus? More often, when word of such instances reaches the principal, an obligatory "wink and nod" conversation with both the perpetrator and victim is considered sufficient. In the minds of many student victims of teacher bullying, the message then becomes clear . . . don't trust adults in the school to remedy the problem!

Camouflaging teacher bullying of students is dangerous for schools on several fronts. On the one hand, students bullied by teachers lose academic focus over fears of retaliation, which often takes the form of lower grades or further abuse. Conversely, teacher bullies feel empowered. They believe their behaviors are validated by institutional inattention, which prompts them to increase the frequency and intensity of their actions. This produces a campus climate of both student fear and intimidation. So is all lost in schools where teacher bullying occurs? Absolutely not. Several strategies to report and combat teacher bullying are available to student victims and sympathetic faculty members:

- *Be aware of where you stand.* Student victims need to do their homework by researching school district policies and regulations regarding bullying. Also, remember that harassment is different from bullying.
- *Be cool.* Students often become very emotional after incidents of teacher bullying. It's not uncommon for victims to approach formal school authorities angry and frustrated. Students should stay calm and practice their messages before meeting with school authorities to ensure they are taken seriously.
- *Understand the concept of two ears and one mouth.* Students who pursue any course of school action after a teacher bullying incident should be aware of the fact that your story will be one of two presented. The perpetrator will also be asked to comment (hopefully at a later date). Responses from school authorities may initially challenge a student's version of the events. By listening more than they speak, victims and supporting adults convince authorities that they are rational, reflective, and not given to exaggeration.
- *Know the end before beginning.* Teacher bullying is a controversial topic and it will be treated as such by school authorities. In many cases, they are interested in "putting the issue to bed" or quickly resolving the problem. Victims and advocates should be aware of possible policy outcomes of the circumstances before the meeting and anticipate explaining things in a clear and concise manner. Be prepared to offer a range of resolutions that

are tied to school policies in order to support your resolve for correcting the problem.
- *Summarize your thoughts.* Students who report teacher bullying should request time during the meeting with the school administration to summarize their feelings surrounding the events of the incident. By being serious and to the point, students gain both credibility and legitimacy in a situation that can be perceived as volatile and prone to interpretation.

The vast majority of adult school personnel are caring and decent people concerned with the well-being of students. Actually, the case can be made that most teachers go beyond the call of their duties and selflessly dedicate their lives to educating young people. Teacher bullies are the exception and not the rule. However, bullying teachers do exist. And just like adult workplace bullies in any organization, unless their behaviors are checked, serious consequences can result from their actions. Although there is still much to be done, many school districts now provide student victims with the structural supports to address such actions. Coupled with the firm resolve of supportive school personnel who listen to the stories of bullied students and react to the dilemmas, inroads into eliminating teacher bullies are being made.

IS THE END IN SIGHT?

Given some of the information contained in this chapter, readers may conclude that there's little hope of eliminating adult bullying, especially without the enactment of anti-bullying laws designed to protect the workplace. There is, however, reason to believe that the problem of adult bullying is gaining the attention of federal lawmakers. Advocates remain vigilant in their attempts to pass the Healthy Workplace Bill, and the legislation has recently gained momentum. Although there is no guarantee that the Healthy Workplace Bill or others like it will be enacted, anti-bullying groups have shed new light on the issue. Time will tell whether their efforts produce a new era where workplace bullying is eliminated.

Coupled with the efforts of concerned private sector anti-bullying activists, an emerging group of students is reacting to teacher bullying in schools. Supported by adult school personnel concerned with eliminating teacher bullying and a host of regulations dedicated to curbing campus aggression, student victims are speaking out in hopes of solving the problem. For example, band "nerds" previously ostracized in classes such as physical education and discarded as less than "jockish" by highly athletic gym teachers have found forums for this harassment via carefully crafted anti-bullying school policies that focus on campus adults who control student classes. Likewise, teachers who witness acts of bullying by other supervising adults also are supported by well-informed faculty colleagues who are aware of the seriousness of these situations.

Adult bullying in both schools and the private sector can be curbed. Concerned leaders and administrators concocting high levels of organizational trust, collegiality, and openness in their workplaces can positively affect the school climate. Remember, workplaces are largely organic, and leaders who replace toxic interactions such as adult bullying with social factors designed to reinforce environments free from predation stand to reap the benefits. Adult bullying of both workplace peers and students deteriorates the social fabric of society, assaults individual dignity, and thefts opportunities at organizational productivity. Arresting the behavior of adult bullies now will ensure that both current and future generations experience much healthier and productive workspaces.

Facts

Just as their youthful counterparts, adult bullies come in many shapes and sizes. Stemming from a wide variety of life experiences, adult bullies generally assume a more sophisticated manner of aggression by choosing to work beneath the public radar in subtler but no less damaging ways. Driven by the need to dominate others, adult bullies in the workplace often resort to lying, spreading rumors about coworkers, and subverting colleagues through personal aggrandizement of their talents at the expense of others.

Coupled with the fact that laws addressing adult bullying are few and far between, many bullies are granted free rein to prowl their workplaces. This gives rise to a number of types of workplace bullies. Due to their insatiable need for victims, the serial bully is widely acknowledged as one of the most deleterious of the adult bullying types. Adult bullies also plague schools, with students often being the targets of bullying teachers. However, in both workplaces and schools there are encouraging signs that action is being taken to quash adult bullying. This includes the introduction of national and state legislation outlining penalties for workplace bullying and more intensified training targeting how to deal with bullying adults.

Feelings

The realization that few workplaces pay heed to adult bullying tactics can be disconcerting. Even more disturbing is the fact that when a bullied stakeholder reports an incident of adult workplace bullying, the victim often is considered an outcast or troublemaker. Although careful documentation and avoiding the bully can assist the case of a victim, being attacked is demoralizing. Adult workplace bullying is indeed a slippery slope and there are no pat answers for solving the dilemma, but there is hope. Take heart in the fact that, akin to teachers bullying students, adult bullies in the workplace who need conflict to maintain their organizational status will eventually overplay their parts and be discovered. Realize that standing up to an adult bully in your workplace will be noticed . . . by the bully and coworkers. Don't hesitate to model appropriate behaviors in light of a bully's abuse! Morality, ethics, and integrity are your allies, and those in the organization who witness your demonstrations of these traits in light of bullying will be encouraged that something can be done!

Facilitation

Adult bullying in both private and school workplaces can be controlled. Leaders who nurture high levels of trust and collegiality in their organizations stand to handsomely benefit from the investment. Toxic work environments conducive to adult bullying can be transitioned to positive places. Through carefully crafted plans to change the climate of the organization, implementing strategic hiring frameworks, and establishing norms that control unwanted behaviors and reward those that are desired, inroads toward eliminating bullying emerge. Dealing effectively with adult bullying in the workplace is much like adhering to the warning signs posted at a railroad crossing: "Stop, look, and listen"! Notice what is happening and what isn't. And realize that, as a leader of an organization that may be plagued by adult bullying, both you and your subordinates will "pay now or pay later" when it comes to eliminating it!

NOTES

1. Fentres (2017).
2. Namie (2010).
3. Einarsen, Hoel, Zapf, and Cooper (2003).
4. Cowie, Neto, Angula, Pereira, Del Barrio, and Ananiadou (2000).
5. Einarsen (2013).
6. Maxwell (2004).
7. Twemlow, Fonagy, Sacco, and Brethour Jr. (2006).

Chapter Four

Mean Streets

An Interview with a Bully

"With a lot of comedians, one of their major attributes is that they look comedic, with a certain hangdog or manic expression. I look like the neighborhood bully. That doesn't elicit laughter."

—Sylvester Stallone

"A young outcast will often feel that there is something wrong with himself, but as he gets older, grows more confident in who he is, he will adapt, he will begin to feel that there is something wrong with everyone else."

—Criss Jami, *Killosophy*

"You either learn to play hard ball or you become the ball."

—Crystal Woods

As is often the case, both authors and editors take considerable pride in presenting to their readers polished exposés elaborating on specific topics of interest. Painstaking care is taken to disseminate thought-provoking information about important subjects in ways that promote ease of understanding. To book lovers, the form and appearance of these materials often determines the success of mixing content with relevance. However, Michael's (pseudonym) story is "unplugged" from stylistic protocols. In fact, he doesn't care all that much about books, or reading, or interviews.

In this chapter, Michael, who is a bully about to graduate from high school, tells his story through his own words . . . right or wrong. While this is exclusively Michael's story, we feel his responses overlay the bullying literature with the unpleasant realities of the life of a bully. Little editing to this transcript has been done so that readers can glean a better understanding of bullying from the bully's perspective—that is, in his own words.

Following the interview with Michael, we present a series of questions for the reader's consideration.

Interviewer: Can you please describe your early childhood and early teenage years?

Michael: I was born in northwestern Ohio. During my childhood, I lived with my grandparents. We didn't have a lot. We lived upstairs in a farmhouse, and my grandparents lived downstairs. We had heat that floated up through open registers in the floor. The whole deal was fairly uneventful, but I always knew we didn't have a lot. I can remember the neighbors bringing food sometimes and putting it on the back steps. We'd find grocery bags of food on the back steps and never knew where it came from.

My dad was a marine. When he got out of the service, we moved into town. My mom worked at a canning factory and peeled tomatoes, and my dad worked with his uncle in a propane gas business. That went belly up when my uncle screwed my dad over. I think he declared bankruptcy. He's never talked about it, but I think he did. So I hit the street when I was probably about eight years old.

My main group of guys that I ran with, we were close. Today we'd be called a gang. A lot of back-alley stuff. Just guys getting together doing stuff out of sight. We lived down by the railroad tracks, so we used to hop the trains when they'd go through. I was 10 years old and I can remember hopping a train for a 10-mile round trip to the stockyard, and we'd run up the stock shoots and jump on the trains when they were going by, and the guys that didn't do it were (expletive).

Interviewer: How would you describe yourself during your earlier years?

Michael: My mom always told me I wasn't the best looking person in the world. My personal perception was I always needed to get better, stronger. I guess part of that was because of my neighborhood. In my neighborhood, there was a lot more physical than mental. Who was stronger? Who was tougher? Who stayed in it longer, if it was fighting? I was thin, lean, and mean. There were bigger guys around, but there were a lot smaller guys, too. My friends probably would say that I was the most mean and most aggressive of the bunch. That helped me where I was growing up, because power was critical in that neighborhood, and it was physical power, which let me run the show for quite a while. People were afraid of me. I've got to be honest with you; I don't mind that.

People at school figured out early on, "Hey, stay away from this guy." They saw the pack that I would run with. I would think that parents probably singled our group out and said stay away from that group there. It was all pretty tough stuff. There were people you messed with and people you didn't. I controlled about four or five guys from my neighborhood. Those were my guys.

Interviewer: There are many who believe low self-esteem encourages individuals to bully. How would you respond to that statement?

Michael: Well, I don't know much about self-esteem. I never thought about it. All I know is what works, and what works is aggressive, being aggressive with people. When people push, I push back twice. That was the way that I got on with things. I didn't think about self-esteem. I'm not a psychologist. I just told you a minute ago, my mom said I wasn't the most attractive guy in the world, and she didn't tell me just once. That may have something to do with it. I don't know; I'm not a psychologist.

Interviewer: Why do you bully?

Michael: Why do I bully? It's a way for me to get what I need. That's all. I don't really feel bad about it. If it doesn't work, I'm going to have to go to something else, but right now, it works, and I do think I get status by bullying folks, shoving my way around. It's a pecking order. You just earn your way up.

Interviewer: What was it like growing up in your family?

Michael: Well, I remember that people were too busy to care. My dad was working two jobs, not only the LP (liquid propane) job, but he used to do plumbing on his own. He used to take me with him, and I can remember my dad crawling under houses in the dead of winter and cleaning out sewage pipes, and the stuff that came out of there wasn't exactly pleasant. I'd crawl under there with him in all the spider webs and dirt. My dad was a grubber. He still is. So Dad wasn't around all that much. My mother probably had more to do with the family. My mom has never been satisfied with anything, including me. I think the way she treats me, and the way we get along, and maybe the way I treat her . . . that doesn't go down too well. In my opinion, I'm not treated very well. My mom has always told me that I'm not good enough. Whatever I do is not good enough. When I was in sports, nothing was ever good enough.

Interviewer: Can you give me an example of what you mean?

Michael: Yeah. I played baseball. I don't anymore. I used to love to play baseball. I was good at it. I was good at pitching. I remember one time, I had just turned 13, there was an all-star game, and I was pitching. My mother was in the stands half way up, right behind home plate. I walked a couple of batters, and she stood up with her fists clenched and out of total silence she screamed at the top of her lungs, "Can't you get the ball over the plate? If you can't do it, don't pitch!"

Interviewer: How did you react?

Michael: I walked the next four batters intentionally. My first pitch after that was three feet over the batter's head, right at her, and then I simply gave up. When I got home, it was the worst. It was all my fault, because I couldn't do what I tried to do, and "she was never going to attend another sporting event of mine for the rest of my life." She was true to her word. I think she just wanted to get out of going. So I gave up on baseball, too. I went to something a little bit harder—fighting, pushing people around, started drinking then. It's not all blame on my mother; everybody's got options. I exercised the options I had. Half the guys in my group told me baseball's for (expletive) anyways, so getting out of it just gave me more time to spend with my guys.

I don't get along with my mom; I just don't, so instead of having these arguments, I just don't go home a lot. I don't miss a lot of school, but a lot of times it's just better if I don't go home. So I just stay at friends' houses. At my house, I'm the bad guy. I have a brother. He's the good kid. He does everything Mom wants him to. We'll see how that works out. My brother and I have grown up under a mother who was a perfectionist, and we were never perfect. That's a big problem. My brother watched me get beat around and slapped, and punched around by my mom. I think he's a little bit intimidated. He just shrinks back and does whatever she tells him, and he's still not good enough for her.

Interviewer: Can you describe what school is like for you?

Michael: I've never had to work at classes. I've had report cards that say, "lack of respect for authority." As a matter of fact, my mother still gets those out and shows those to me. The other thing that's always on my report card, "performing under ability." Some of my teachers have told my parents, "He's extremely bright, but he won't work at it." I don't (expletive) around with these clowns at the top that want to know their class rankings every day. I don't give a (expletive) about that. I get Bs, Cs. I never study. What it's become lately is just "control him." Let him get the grades he gets as long as he doesn't step out of line. I've had a couple of teachers that have taken me aside and given me the "you can do better" speech. And I give them the "I don't give a (expletive)" response, and they give up. Maybe that's my way of bullying them; I don't know.

Interviewer: What about earlier on, in elementary school, what was that like?

Michael: Elementary school was pretty uneventful. I cruised through it. In second grade, I broke an aquarium and my teacher made me sit in the wastebasket the whole day, and I was really embarrassed about that.

Interviewer: Did you break it intentionally?

Michael: No. I was with a friend of mine. We were being punished with no recess and we were messing around with it at noon when no one was in the room, and all of a sudden it broke, but we weren't trying to break it. The principal came down and paddled us. We went to the restroom and laughed our (expletive) off.

Interviewer: What about middle school?

Michael: When I went into junior high, I saw there was immediately a pecking order. Most of it was based on sports and athletic ability. That's when the baseball incident happened. I saw early on that if you were on the baseball team, basketball team, you were somebody, so I played basketball, and I tried football. That didn't work because of the nature of the football coaches. I clashed with their personalities right away. They were going to show me the way, bring me under their control, and that wasn't going to work for me. Even on the football field, I was always roughing people up, pushing people out of the way. I think that's where the conflict with the coaching staff came in. None of them ever talked to me about channeling my aggression. It was always, "Sit on the bench! You're a hothead! Don't get in anybody's face like that! I'll tell you what to do!" And that didn't work for me, so sports were short-lived in my life.

I had my first girlfriend in junior high. Pam and I were together for years. I don't know how it worked, but it worked. We ran in a different group. My guys in my neighborhood, we kind of broke up for a while there, some of them moved to better neighborhoods. We'd see each other at school and were always good friends, but I started running with the elite athletes, and we all had girlfriends, and we'd go to each other's houses, blow smoke at each other. Dating Pam helped me get out of the place I'd been for a while . . . for a while.

When I dropped out of sports my sophomore year, I went right back to my old ways. I had a school reputation that I could have been a good athlete, but because of what they called, "the way he is," I got pushed out of sports, or I quit sports, whatever you want to call it. Something had to fill my time up, so what I had then was a group of athletes who were everything in my small town. They were the stars, so I would push back against them. The same people that I had been teammates with, now I pushed back against them, because in my mind I had thought that I had been refused by that group.

At that time, the coaches were the worst. The size of our school, and my reputation. I didn't have any room at all, and I didn't care. I would walk down the halls and I would be the only person walking down the halls, and the coaches would be coming toward me, they would stop and look away at the opposite wall until I had passed and then they would keep walking.

Interviewer: Do you remember any other interactions at school?

Michael: One story sticks in my mind that I will never forget. (Expletive.) In basketball, I averaged 24 points per game my freshman year. When I quit, I remember, I'd stay after school and I'd just go to the gym and shoot around. And one day, the head football coach came in and he said, "Why are you here?" And I said, "Why shouldn't I be here?" It was after school. And the head football coach was everything in that small town, everything. He said, "Why are you here? You think you're too good to play on our teams. You quit basketball and football, and you shouldn't be using this gym." And I said, "I've got every right to use the gym; the team's not using it." He said, "I want you out of here, and I want you out of here now."

So I got the ball, and I started walking toward the door. And the weight room was on an elevated area above where I was walking, and as I walked by the weight room, the weight coach spit on me from up above. So I walked out. The next day I had to go to the principal's office. That incident was a big change for me. I went to the principal's office—Mr. Clark's office—and he wasn't bad at all. He said, "Why do you do the things you do?" And I started talking about the incident, and he said, "No, it's bigger than that; your whole life you're pushing limits, pushing folks around, why is that?" I said, "I don't know, I guess it's the only way I can get anything done." He said, "Do me a favor, just for me, come and talk to me any time you want about anything you want, and here's what I'm asking you to do . . . try not to be as much the way you are. Just try not to be the way you are as much as you are." I said, "All right, I'll give it a shot." I left. A week later, the coaches were on my ass again; I went to him, and it was like he never talked to me.

Interviewer: Any other incidents at school you'd like to talk about?

Michael: I let a bunch of students into a Friday night dance. I opened up a side door and about 50 kids came in free instead of paying admission. One of the teachers caught me, and I could tell right away he was afraid of me. He said, "I want you to know I have no respect for you." I just looked at him and said, "Well, that hurts my feelings a lot," and I walked away.

Interviewer: All in all, would you say your early school experience was a rocky road?

Michael: Things are what they are. Never thought about it.

Interviewer: What methods do you use when you bully other kids?

Michael: The way I'm hard-wired and the way my neighborhood is structured, we've already talked about this—when people get in my way, I use physical things to get them out of my way. I don't blindside people, 'cause that's what (expletive) do. I always tell people where things are going. If that doesn't work, I take it to the next step, which is physical. That's always worked for me.

If I punch somebody now, everybody knows who punched somebody. So my reputation works two ways. It does what I want to do, lets me be known how I want to be known, but if there's a fight out in the parking lot, if something's stolen, the first person they call in is me. So it cuts both ways. It's a double edge. I will tell you, I don't think I'm a dumb person. Grades aside, I've got street smarts and I've done okay in the classroom. I could do better, but I choose how I want to live my life. I play angles now more than I used to. In junior high, it was pure force, followed by words, "Don't do that again." Now it's words first because of my reputation, and most of the time, people just stay away from me, and I don't have to do anything.

Interviewer: Can you talk more about your interaction with friends and peers?

Michael: I lost my original gang in mid-junior high. We didn't hang out as much, 'cause I was with another group . . . the jocks. During high school, we came back together again. I love those guys. They're like brothers to me. But what happens is that when we go out now, I'm the bully and somewhat of a leader, but I'm also the protector of the rest of the group. There are bullies in every town . . . everywhere. In every town we go to, we cross paths. We go to other schools' high school dances. It doesn't take long to find trouble. The energy's there; it's always there. We have some guys in my group, they're not exactly physically strong, so when we go into foreign territory like other towns, the weaker ones in my bunch are always the ones that get picked on right away. Then my role is to protect my guys from being hammered, so on one hand we're out there looking for someone for me to hammer, but don't do the same thing and pick on my guys. It's kind of weird.

I feel kind of weird calling myself a bully, actually. It just doesn't sit well with me. This is just who I am, but the other people you are calling bullies . . . it's a competitive thing. And I end up protecting my guys.

Interviewer: What term would you use?

Michael: I don't know if I have a term; I'm me. That's it. I'm pretty comfortable with who I am. My mother always used to use a term, she'd say, "I'm not going to wear the hair shirt." I don't know what that means, but I guess that's her way of saying, "I'm not going to take the blame." You hear bullying used as a really negative word; I don't see it that way. This is just who I am.

Interviewer: What do you get out of bullying?

Michael: The reason I bullied, and maybe I still do, is it's my way to success. Plus, I've been involved with this stuff so long, in a town the size of ours, whether it's a school or a community, or friends, or other kids' families, everybody knows. So the frame is set, the die is cast. I am who I am and I've got this reputation, and unless I move out or move on, or get some kind of weepy church thing and have a conversion, it's there, and that's the way it's going to be.

Interviewer: Were you ever sorry about bullying people?

Michael: Do I feel bad about it? Not in the least. Other people play games to compete. Some people sit around and play chess. I've got to be aggressive with people to see who wins. Very rarely do I feel bad. On occasion, I have thought about some specific incidents where I took advantage of people—involving people with handicaps. It's kind of weird because when I get into it with people, I guess it's a sense of pride that I want to get into it with people who deserved to be hassled. Most of the time, they're jocks, or people who think they're better than I am, or people that are bullying other people. That's my game. When I see people in my gang that are bullying other weaker people, I tend to jump in and take charge of that, so I bully the bully. But the times I've had second thoughts are when I've said things or done things to handicapped people.

Interviewer: And those are the ones you feel guilty about?

Michael: Yeah, 'cause it didn't make me feel any better, and I didn't accomplish anything by picking on someone who was weaker or crippled. Most of the trouble I get into is with people who were as strong or stronger than me, 'cause I want people to recognize me.

Interviewer: What advice would you give to bullies or victims of bullying?

Michael: Well, I'm not done with it yet. (Laughter.) It's not as easy as people think. I don't walk down the school halls trying to push people around. It just kind of happens the way I see a situation. It just kind of unfolds. If I had a do over, I'd change some things, but right now, I'll tell you I don't think I'd be any more successful. What I can't get out of my mind, is if I take myself back five or six years ago, if I hadn't done that or stayed here, or done that, how much better off would I be? I can't convince myself I'd be any better off.

Maybe it's a mind-set that says if I had done all they wanted me to, I'd be a (expletive), and I still wouldn't have anything, so what would I advise other people? The law is coming. That's what. I can see it in my own situation. It used to be where like the principal would call me in and talk to me, then guidance counselors, and they'd call you in and talk, or my old man would call the pastor, and he would talk to you, but it's getting bigger than that now. So what I'd say to other bullies, the game's changing.

It's getting a lot rougher. The police get involved, you're getting laws and rules, and you're probably going to do time now. Whether it's JDC (Juvenile Detention Center), or you're really going to go to jail. I've seen a change. Maybe pushing someone isn't going to do it anymore. You've got to do more to get your point across. I'm a little older now; people know who I am. Unless I get out of here, I'm either going to find a job, or possibly something bad's going to happen . . . and possibly something good's going to happen. I don't bully as much as I used to. Maybe it's getting old, maybe I'm getting older, but the game is changing.

Interviewer: Anything else you want to add?

Michael: I got the feeling that there's some kind of sob story you're looking for. I don't want anybody to think that. Do I regret my life? People say there's a life wasted. I don't feel that way at all. I've told you how I grew up, but I don't want anybody feeling sorry for me. I really don't; it's just the way life works out.

I would say something I've noticed the last few years, the group I grew up with, they are still as loyal to me, and I to them as the day we pulled together. And I don't see a lot of that in other circles. But I'll go to the wall for them, and they'll go to the wall for me.

If you're going to push people around, you're going to spend a lot of time doing it; if you can do something else, go do it. You never know when you're going to meet me, or somebody like me, and I live with the same deal. I never know who I'm going to meet when I do these things, it just takes a lot of time and a lot of energy. I guess other people put their energy into being a football player, or what do you call it, student government? If you're going to do what I do, it takes time and energy to be good at it. That's all I have to say.

DISCUSSING THE INTERVIEW

1. To what degree do you feel bullies are products of their environments? Are they exclusively responsible for their own choices? What evidence do

you see in this interview (or in your own life experiences) that leads you to this conclusion?

2. What surprised you about Michael's interview?
3. What actions would you take if you were Michael's parent, teacher, or principal?
4. Based on your personal impressions of the interview, what missed opportunities can you identify that may have changed Michael's situation? By extension, what opportunities do you feel exist for your school to improve bullying mitigation efforts?
5. Were you ever bullied? Given the opportunity, what questions would you ask the person who bullied you?

Facts

Whether victimizing peers, subordinates, or those in perceived positions of authority, bullies attempt to exercise serious control over others when they engage their victims. Unfortunately, Michael's case is not exceptional, and numerous factors such as a bully's social background, home life, and early incidences of bullying success combine to form reinforcing mechanisms, which perpetuate aggressive actions by bullies.

Feelings

In the wake of campus bullying incidents, organizational stakeholders often experience high degrees of anger, frustration, and fear. Indeed, these post-incident emotions are commonly linked to the frequency of bullying occurrences, personalities in play, and timely actions initiated by institutional authorities designed to stem future incidences of victimization. As Michael's story reveals, many factors influence the actions and behaviors of a bully, and campus leaders are challenged to control a complex array of social situations resulting from their actions. However, savvy school authorities recognize that failing to address the emotional fallout accompanying acts of bullying simply aids and abets future disturbances. Disarming the harmful effects of prevailing institutional emotions by listening carefully to your people and responding expeditiously to their concerns help keep the situation manageable!

Facilitation

There are no quick fixes to the problems associated with bullying. As demonstrated in Michael's interview, the interplay of many factors beyond the reach of the school precipitates the bully mind-set. Unfortunately, bullies leave school leaders to deal with a combination of social assets that produce aggressive and antisocial actions. One important key to managing student bullying is recognizing that the task is multifaceted and responsibilities for addressing the problem are not exclusively that of the school. Yet it's true that the immediate issue is providing safe schooling for students. This means targeting, confronting, and removing the problem(s) from campus by enlisting the help of a core group of well-trained school professionals. Formulate this "inner circle" unit from proven and trusted campus veterans who have earned the respect of both school and community stakeholders. In addition, designate a key member of your administrative staff to locate, log, and establish contact with all community support services available to assist you. And reach out to these agencies before you need them! Finally, pledge to make your planning proactive rather than reactive. Have your system ready for action and never attempt to build an anti-bullying "bridge" as you walk on it!

Chapter Five

Tactics and Responses for Victims of Bullying

"(He) is like most big bullies. If you can stay away and make him miss for a few rounds, he'll get frustrated. Once you strip away that feeling of invincibility, he can be had."

—Rocky Marciano, former heavyweight boxing champion

"No one can make you feel inferior without your consent."

—Eleanor Roosevelt

Rocco Francis Marchegiano was never the biggest kid on the block. After dropping out of high school in grade 10, he worked odd jobs as a delivery man, a ditch digger, a railroad layer, and a shoemaker. At the age of 25, he decided he wanted to become a professional boxer. He fought some amateur fights and worked out in front of boxing trainers. Goody Petronelli was one of the trainers who watched Mr. Marchegiano in the ring. When asked what he thought of this aspiring boxer's prospects, Petronelli said he'd never make it. He was too short, too old, too light, and his arms weren't long enough. He had no reach. How could he possibly compete against other boxers who were bigger and stronger than him?

Despite this inauspicious beginning, this late bloomer was about to prove all his critics wrong. He began competing as a professional boxer in 1947. Because a ringside announcer had trouble pronouncing his name, he simplified it—to Rocky Marciano. Rocky won his first professional fight, and the next, and the next. In 1952, he defeated Joe Lewis to become the heavyweight champion, a title he never relinquished. In fact, Rocky Marciano is the only heavyweight champion to go undefeated in his career. Years later, when a sportswriter asked Marciano about fighting a younger, stronger opponent,

Rocky replied, "(He) is like most big bullies. If you can stay away and make him miss for a few rounds, he'll get frustrated. Once you strip away that feeling of invincibility, he can be had."

Rocky understood that no matter how big or intimidating an enemy might appear, if he could find a way to avoid his attacks, he could neutralize his opponent's strength. The research on bullying victimization is important to understand so that we can learn how to build up safeguards against bullying. One of the most important buffers that reduce the likelihood of becoming a bullying victim has to do with social encounters. As children in their formative years interact with others, these encounters influence their development in both positive and negative ways. When social encounters are positive, children develop stress-reducing behaviors. When their early encounters are negative, the likelihood of becoming victims of bullying increases.[1]

Individuals who have close and positive relationships with their mothers tend to report lower incidents of bullying than their peers.[2] However, individuals who experience maternal overprotection or intrusiveness report higher levels of bully victimization.[3] So mothers should be involved, but not overprotect or become intrusive. What about dads? Fathers also play an important role in combating a child's propensity to be bullied. Children who perceive their fathers as significant role models in their lives report less bullying than those who have low levels of involvement with their dads.[4]

Relationships with friends are also a crucial buffer against bullying. Students who have fewer friends experience higher levels of bullying than students who have more friends.[5] Interestingly, although victims of bullying tend to have fewer friendships, the relationships they do have are extremely significant to them.[6] It's important to note that strong relationships with parents or friends are not a guarantee that bullying will not occur—what these relationships do provide is a buffer against bullying. But what if bullying is already occurring?

WHAT YOU CAN DO ABOUT IT

Realize the Value of Self-Worth

If you know a child who is currently a victim of bullying, it is important for them to know that there are many other people out there who have suffered as they have. Many of them have gone on to accomplish amazing things. It's our hope that victims will draw strength in reading the stories of other bullying survivors. One of those individuals is Batman. Well, not Batman exactly, but the actor who portrayed Batman.

Christian Bale was intensely bullied when he was in school. In an interview with *People* magazine, he said, "I took a beating from several boys for years. They put me through hell, punching and kicking me all the time." He has this advice for people who may be experiencing bullying: "If you can face the bullying at school and come through it stronger, that is a lesson for life." It can be difficult to believe that the way things are in elementary, middle, or high school are not the way things will always be; however, the possible future successes for victims of bullying who persevere are limitless. It is likely that none of the bullies who were picking on Christian Bale would have guessed he would grow up to become a superhero.

Seek Out a Support System of Peers

Not all of us can be Batman. There will always be times when you are not the biggest or the strongest person in the room. But power isn't only derived from muscle mass. At times, mind-set can be even more powerful. Eleanor Roosevelt once said, "No one can make you feel inferior without your consent." Think about that for a minute. Someone might hit you, mock you, or spit on you, but they can't make you feel inferior—how you feel about yourself is up to you. Eleanor Roosevelt is the United States' longest serving first lady. She used this platform to speak up for women's rights, civil rights, and respect for veterans.

One of the most impactful moments in her time as first lady came during a veterans' protest march in Washington, DC. Following World War I, many veterans were not able to find work due to the Great Depression. This hardship was acknowledged by Congress, who passed the World War Adjusted Compensation Act of 1924 that awarded bonuses to veterans—but the catch was that these bonuses could not be cashed in until 1945. This angered many veterans who had been out of work, and so they marched together on Washington demanding that their compensation not be delayed by 21 years. The first of these protest marches occurred before the Roosevelt administration. The response from then president Herbert Hoover was to send the army to disperse the protestors.

In 1933, there was a second protest marching for the same cause. This time, instead of sending in the army, Franklin Delano Roosevelt sent his wife, who met with the veterans, listened to their concerns, sang songs with them, and diffused the tension, working out a temporary solution offering veterans jobs in the Civilian Conservation Corps. If bullying exists due to power differentials, then it is hard to imagine a much more powerful bully than the federal government, but when tens of thousands of veterans banded together to say a 21-year delay in compensation was unacceptable, this most powerful of enemies relented. Finally, in 1936, Congress voted to pay the veterans' bonuses nine years early.

Just as this group of veterans chose a unified direction by banding together with their peers, so, too, bully victims have a choice. They have the option of choosing isolation, which only sets them up for further victimization, or they can choose to befriend a larger group of peers, which insulates the entire group from further persecution.

Avoid Bullying Hot Spots

When someone is being bullied, a temptation can be to skip school in order to avoid the bullying altogether. As reported earlier, approximately 160,000 students skip school every day because of bullying.[7] The problem with school avoidance is that it is the victim whose learning suffers. In fact, researchers have found that victims of bullying not only have higher rates of school avoidance, they also do not perform as well academically as their non-bullied peers.[8]

Another option in avoiding bullies is to consider the exact times of day, day of the week, and location on campus where bullying is occurring. For instance, if bullying is happening before school starts, would it be possible to arrive later, or to get permission to stay in the library before school starts? If bullying is happening in the boys' bathroom, would it be possible to find a different restroom, or ask an adult for permission to use the bathroom in the front office? If bullying happens at the lockers, would it be possible to request a different locker assignment? Avoiding times and places where bullying is likely to occur can be an important deterrent in reducing the likelihood of bullying incidents.

Speak Up

If peers or teachers know someone whom they suspect may be the victim of bullying, there's a lot they can do to help. First, a peer or teacher could invite them to be a part of their group. This could be as simple as saying, "Why don't you sit with us at lunch today," or engaging someone in conversation as you walk from one class to the next. Bullies are far less likely to target someone who is a part of a larger group.

Jackie Chan has performed in dozens of Hollywood movies such as *Rush Hour*, *The Forbidden Kingdom*, and as the voice of the Monkey in *Kung Fu Panda*. It's hard to imagine this martial arts expert being bullied, but that is in fact the case. What broke the cycle of bullying for Chan was when he decided to stand up for someone else. Jackie relays the story this way, "I was bullied quite a lot when I was growing up. . . . I allowed myself to be bullied because I was scared and I didn't know how to defend myself."

The next year at school, there was a new crop of underclassmen who were even easier to pick on, so the bullies turned some of their attention to the new students. One day, Jackie found himself watching a friend being bullied, and he decided to act. Instead of watching the incident as others had watched him be bullied, Jackie took the opportunity to stand up to the same group who had once bullied him. This is when he stopped allowing himself to be a victim. In his own words, "By standing up for him, I learned to stand up for myself." Chan's example provides another option in responding to bullying.

Victims can either speak out in their own defense, or in the defense of others. Safe spaces are made available for a victim witnessing what they have gone through in which they feel more comfortable championing another's plight than their own. This advocacy for others offers multiple benefits by allowing a former victim to be in a position of strength, while also spotlighting their own predicament. By advocating for others, victims can often experience a renewed sense of self, thereby reducing the chance of further bullying.

Find an Adult Who Cares

If students do not feel safe speaking up to the bully directly, they should speak up by telling an adult who cares. This could be a teacher, a counselor, an administrator, or any other adult on campus. They should let an adult know they have a concern, and then follow up with them if the situation doesn't improve. Don't think that by speaking up the student's job is done. They should keep seeking out help until the situation improves. Most important, students should not be silent bystanders.

New York Times best-selling author Dr. Robert Cialdini writes about the concept of social persuasion. He notes that people look to one another to decide how they should respond to circumstances.[9] This is particularly important for those who witness a bullying situation. Often, when there are conflicts at school, crowds gather, watch, and do little to intervene. This is not because the bystanders are inherently cruel; they are simply behaving the way that humans behave—looking to others to see how they should respond. It's social persuasion. Individuals who are looking to stop bullying can make a difference by finding an adult who cares.

Bullying affects students of all backgrounds. Multiple studies have shown that regardless of race, ethnicity, or socioeconomic status, the impact of bullying is the same.[10] One fact is clear: Bullying does not discriminate. It occurs in poor schools, it occurs in rich schools, it occurs in monochromatic schools, and it occurs in multiracial schools. From the perspective of one bullying victim, a factor that helped him survive his tormentors was having a support system.

Entertainer Chris Rock is one of the most successful standup comedians in the world. After beginning his career in comedy as a cast member of *Saturday Night Live* in the 1990s, Chris Rock has gone on to star in multiple films, host the Academy Awards, and was voted one of the top five comedians of all time in a poll conducted by Comedy Central. An interviewer on BET asked Chris Rock about his life before he became famous. "We lived in Bed-Stuy, one of the most famous ghettos in the world. My mother and father wanted me to go to a better school, so I was bused to this poor white neighborhood . . . I was the only black boy in my grade. . . . I was a little guy . . . a skinny runt." He says bullies "kicked my ass, spit in my face, and kicked me down the stairs."

Chris Rock sees being bullied as the defining moment in his life. "It made me who I am," he said, adding, "But you need love too. . . . Bullying without love? You can be destroyed. But you know, I was bullied and I had love at home." From the perspective of this bullying victim, the way he was able to survive was thanks to the support of others. Thus an important lesson for people who may be reading this book who are current victims of bullying (or know someone who is currently the victim of bullying) is this: Seek out support of others. This may be a parent, a teacher, a counselor, or a school administrator.

STRAIGHT FROM THE HEADLINES

In middle school, many kids feel awkward. For some, pointing out other people's deficiencies can take the focus off their own insecurities. When those behaviors go unchecked, the school environment can become unsafe. Such was the case at Winch Middle School in South Glens Falls, Florida. With 86 reported incidents of bullying or harassment occurring within one school year, this campus had one of the highest levels of bullying reported for the state of Florida.

According to Jonathon Stewart, a student at Winch, the culture of bullying had found a foothold there. Specifically, the bullying witnessed by Jonathon had to do with sexuality and gender identity. He says some kids at school were merciless when it came to boys behaving "like boys" and quickly hurled slurs at anyone who didn't. "It happens at my lunch table all the time," he said in a story reported by the *Times Union* newspaper, boys were, "calling people 'faggot' and 'gay.' . . . Being a guy in this school, growing up, you're definitely self-conscious. And if you stand up for the gays or anybody, you become the target."[11]

One of the boys that Jonathon saw being picked on was Jacobe Taras. A bit of a late bloomer compared to his middle school friends, Jacobe was just becoming interested in girls. His tardiness made him the target of anti-gay slurs.

One day, a school counselor passed forms out to all the middle school students. The form had simple check-boxes to indicate if anyone had anything they wanted to talk to the counselor about. Jacobe Taras checked off "no," then scratched it off, and wrote beside it, "maybe." Unfortunately, no one followed up with Jacobe Taras—and two weeks later, he took his own life. Here is what he wrote in his suicide note (figure 5.1):

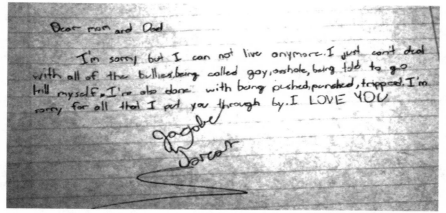

Figure 5.1. Suicide Note Written by Jacobe Taras
Source: Bump, B. (2016, May 28). Parents sue South Glens Falls schools after bullied son kills himself. *Times Union.* Retrieved from http://www.timesunion.com/tuplus-local/article/Parents-sue-South-Glens-Falls-schools-after-7951546.php

How schools react to incidents like these can be a turning point, engaging all stakeholders to ensure that incidents like this never happen again. Unfortunately, many schools choose not to engage in these difficult conversations, opting instead to bury the incident. This appears to be the case at Winch, where administrators told students the young teen had been in a hunting accident.

This lack of willingness to address bullying angers Jacobe's parents. "They hide behind this line of, 'Oh, another student was involved so we couldn't tell you anything in order to protect their privacy,'" said Richard Taras, Jacobe's father. "Well, you don't have to give us names. But we should know when our children are being violated." "They hide it underneath the carpet," said Christine Taras. "They don't want to acknowledge it."[12] Is your school doing all it can to address bullying, or is it just going through the motions?

Table 5.1. Dos and Don'ts for Bullying Victims

Do:	Don't:
Realize the value of self-worth	Blame yourself
Seek out a support system of peers	Stay quiet
Avoid bullying hot spots	Hurt yourself
Speak up	Think you are alone
Find an adult who cares	Stop asking for help

CONNECTIONS WITH THE BULLYING RESEARCH

Researchers have found that victims of bullying experience both lower levels of social acceptance and self-worth than non-bullied students.[13] Even more alarming are the long-term effects. Repercussions of victimization often persist beyond school years, and victims exhibit symptoms of bullying well into adulthood.[14] The lingering negative effects of bullying can take many forms, including depression, loneliness, and anxiety.[15]

Finding effective solutions to bullying is never easy, and it would be overly idealistic to believe that any individual can completely stop all bullying. However, there are many strategies that schools, communities, parents, bystanders, and victims can exercise in order to stand up against bullying. See table 5.1 for a concise overview of the recommendations that were presented in this chapter regarding what you can do if you find yourself being bullied.

Facts

- Bullying affects students of all backgrounds.
- Students who have fewer friends among their peer groups experience higher levels of bullying than students who have more friends.
- People look to one another to decide how they should respond to situations.

Feelings

Realize the value of self-worth. Although it's likely hard to believe it at the time, this is just one stage in your life. You have the potential to accomplish great things, and your life is of value.

Facilitation

It may be tempting to withdraw from your friends when you're bullied. Don't! When you are alone, you can become an easier target for future bullying. By withdrawing from your friends, you are allowing the bully to win. Instead, seek out a support system of peers.

Avoid bullying hot spots. If there are certain times of day, or certain locations within the school where bullying most frequently occurs, look for an easy way to avoid these areas.

Speak up. This could mean speaking up for yourself, or for someone else. Remember Jackie Chan. Before he became a martial arts star, he was smaller than most other kids, and he was picked on. As he grew older, the bullies found younger victims. Just like there will always be people bigger and stronger than you, there will also be people smaller and weaker than you. Consider what you can do to make their lives better.

Finally, seek out an adult who cares. Most people who work in schools choose their career path because they want to help people. Many educators refer to their career as a calling, or a service profession. If you happen to encounter an educator who is burned out or doesn't seem to care, find a different adult. Most important, don't stop asking for help until you find it and remember that you are the only one who gets to decide how you feel about yourself. In the words of Eleanor Roosevelt, "No one can make you feel inferior without your consent."

NOTES

1. Conners-Burrow, Johnson, Whiteside-Mansell, McKelvey, and Gargus (2009).
2. Beran and Violato (2004).
3. Paul (2006).
4. Flouri and Buchanan (2002).
5. Perren and Alsaker (2006).
6. Goldbaum, Craig, Pepler, and Connoly (2003).
7. Van Roeckel (2012).
8. Hanish and Guerra (2002); Rueger, Malecki, and Demaray (2011).
9. Cialdini, 2006).
10. Cooper (2011).
11. Bump (2016).
12. Bump (2016).
13. Mouttapa, Valent, Gallaher, Rohrbach, and Unger (2004).
14. Kochenderfer-Ladd and Wardrop (2001).
15. Hodges, Boivin, Vitaro, and Bukowski (1999); Swearer, Song, Cary, Eagle, and Mickelson (2001).

Chapter Six

Bystanders and the Role of Peers

"The world is a dangerous place, not because of those who do evil, but because of those who look on and do nothing."

—Albert Einstein

"Silence in the face of evil is itself evil: God will not hold us guiltless. Not to speak is to speak. Not to act is to act."

—Dietrich Bonhoeffer, author of *The Cost of Discipleship*

"After all there are no innocent bystanders. What are they doing here in the first place?"

—William S. Burroughs, author of *Naked Lunch*

The introduction to this book draws an analogy between fishing and bullying. Readers interested in stopping bullying were acquainted with an angling technique fishermen use called "matching the hatch" or recognizing that each stream is unique, knowing exactly what specific insects the trout in any given stream are eating, and the circumstances surrounding the fish's habitat. Likewise, we proposed that school personnel concerned with stopping bullying could learn a thing or two from the angling world by closely scrutinizing the environments of their campuses and studying the attributes of the stakeholders. In other words, we advocated that the more intimately aware of the campus environment school personnel become, the greater the opportunity for a successful anti-bullying effort.

If we return to the trout fishing example described earlier in the book, we'll find there's a distinctly different way of viewing the same situation. Although our example illustrates that anglers who "read" the stream can leverage their fishing successes by carefully observing the environment, we neglected to mention that serious undertakings are simultaneously occurring under the water's surface as predacious trout force baitfish and weaker prey into hazardous encounters. As opposed to what anglers see and analyze above the surface, it's a different game below as voracious trout lie in wait for a school of unsuspecting minnows to pass. When the attack is launched on the unwary baitfish, the trout usually single out one or two for lunch while the remainder of the minnows simply floats idly by.

Similarly, school personnel who view the campus from the vantage of a secure hallway or quiet corridor frequently assume that students are immune from predation. But like trout that are familiar with subsurface ambush spots of a stream, bullies also see and use school territory differently than campus authorities. Just as concerned school personnel determine areas and situations where bullying can be prevented, so, too, bullies often calculate where, when, and how to prey on their unsuspecting victims.

To that end, bullies often operate under the surface and perpetrate in the shadows of the adult world. They impact the campus environment in reckless and negative ways far removed from sources of school authority. And as in the case of an opportunistic trout hidden in the recesses of a stream's ambush points, bullies also locate cloistered school areas to assault weak, isolated, and unsuspecting students without fear of intervention by others.

Consistently monitoring all areas of the school makes many campus authorities feel like prison wardens or commandants. They lament that although after-the-fact reports indicate many students and staff witnessed the bullying, no one seemed to step up and intervene in the incident. Remember our example? After the trout has isolated its prey, the remainder of the minnows simply floats idly by. Unfortunately student bystanders to bullying incidents often mime the reaction of a school of baitfish to a trout's predation . . . as long as the bullying doesn't affect them, they stand idly by. Thus, having previously discussed bullies and their victims, we now turn to bystanders, the third integral group involved in the bullying triad. This chapter will consider the question of how the actions (or inaction) of bystanders in response to bullying circumstances affect them, their peers, and those who bully.

BULLYING: THREE LINKS IN THE SAME CHAIN

Most school leaders view bullying as a two-person encounter featuring the perpetrator and the victim. That's because bullying incidents are immediate and visceral. The victim's health and safety are at stake, and intervention usually is necessitated by the occurrence. Bullies and victims take center stage.

However, even those who aren't active players in the incident are still affected. Based on their observances and reactions to the events, witnesses can become victims, participants, or defenders. In fact, bullying usually involves three parties: bully, victim, and bystanders.

There are three links in the bullying chain, and the strength or robustness of each link oftentimes determines where informed school administrators dedicate their anti-bullying efforts. For example, if bullying on campus is overt, immediate steps are taken to both eliminate the occurrences and protect the students. Let's face it: from a school and community perspective, that which is seen as detrimental is most often addressed, and pursuing a stop gap course of action is just plain rational. It "stops the bleeding" when it comes to effectively dealing with the problems at hand.

There does exist another important (and often neglected) link in the bullying chain. Those who see bullying happen or hear about it represent a strong resource available to anti-bullying forces. Although often viewed as ancillary to actual bullying incidents, bystanders also are affected by what they witness. Admittedly, the effects on this group are outwardly more subtle and potentially more diverse, but they are no less important. In fact, how campus leaders deal with this group in the aftermath of a bullying incident weighs heavily into whether or not school anti-bullying initiatives are taken seriously.

Most of us are acquainted with the expression "a chain is only as strong as its weakest link." The bullying link is at its weakest when witnesses refuse to stand idly by. By properly supporting both the victim and bystanders, school leaders can go a long way toward breaking the bullying chain.

BULLYING AND BYSTANDERS:
THE DISEASE PARALLEL

For anyone investigating the bullying literature, it comes as no surprise to find the subject is often compared to a disease. Most certainly, the phenomenon does represent a social malady that merits professional attention. That said, some interesting parallels do come to mind when comparing bullying to a serious illness. For example, bullying is similar to cancer in that once it materializes it disrupts the course of the victim's life by depleting energy, challenging his or her physical stamina, and jeopardizing mental stability.

Akin to the insidious ability of cancer to metastasize, if left unchecked, bullying can—and will—spread. However, unlike cancer, whose deadly reach is confined to one victim, bullying holds the potential to spread its toxic effects to those beyond the initial target. Acts of bullying in the presence of bystanders prompt lasting effects for bullies, victims, and those watching.

Bystanders exposed to bullying incidents often find themselves between the proverbial rock and a hard place when it comes to reacting. Although research indicates that bystander intervention in a bullying incident within 10 seconds of exposure can effectively stop the occurrence, that's not normally the case. Bystander interventionists are definitely in the minority. So what's up? Why don't more bystanders react to bullies? In truth, several factors determine how bystanders react to bullying situations. Some can be very helpful in stopping incidents, while others exacerbate the act.

BYSTANDERS: LOOKING THROUGH
THE BENT-BACKED TULIPS?

Among other whimsical lyrics, the late John Lennon's song "Glass Onion" contains the lines "Looking through the bent-backed tulips. To see how the other half live." The reference is to a not-so-fortunate person, who gazes over at the affluent dining clientele through the lush flower displays at Parkes, a then-fashionable restaurant on London's Beauchamp Place. Most certainly, bystanders to bullying aren't peering through the "bent-backed tulips" when they witness bullying, but they do share impassivity in common with Lennon's observer. Like the wishful diner in the song, bystanders view the activity, but by and large don't participate. Why is this the case? Several reasons exist for why bystanders don't intervene in bullying episodes.

- *They don't feel it's their business.* Not understanding what happened to precipitate the incident is often enough cause for bystanders to abstain from assisting the victim.
- *The fear of retribution by the bully stymies their desires to help.* Many bystanders feel that remaining on the sidelines prevents them from becoming the bully's next target.
- *The frustration experienced over previously unsuccessful reporting to responsible adults.* Based on past experiences, bystanders believe telling adults won't impact the situation.
- *A general feeling of powerlessness takes precedence over action.* Although certain bystanders to bullying may want to intervene, they feel powerless in light of the bully's size and aggressiveness.
- *A lack of education about bullying situations and intervention strategies promotes noninvolvement.* Some bystanders simply don't know how to respond. Thus, their ignorance leads to paralysis.
- *The volatility of the situation promotes passivity.* Most students on campus opt to "see and not be seen." Therefore, they watch the incident and avoid drawing attention to themselves through an intervention.

- *The perceived reputation of the victim precludes bystanders from getting involved.* Whether deserved or not, many students on campus have reputations that aren't encouraging. Certain bystanders who are aware of these student tags feel the victimization is warranted and, consequently, fail to intervene in the situation.

While others involved in the anti-bullying movement may consider these reasons as excuses for nonintervention, bystanders justify their inaction by them. A critical issue confronting both schools and communities exposed to bullying is how to ensure the majority of bystanders proactively and decisively intervenes on behalf of victims. *The answer lies in delivering a clear, concise, and affirming message to bystanders that both action and intervention are effective responses to bullying.* Adults with the credibility, training, conviction, and authority to resoundingly act on such pronouncements must take the lead on delivering this message! When this is the case, bystander empowerment is legitimized, and reasons for not intervening in bullying situations become trite and minimal.

Unfortunately, many school leaders interested in eliminating bullying from their campuses have a long way to go in forwarding bystander empowerment through organizational support mechanisms. Thus, administrative inconsistency in supporting bystander interventions often fuels confusion about whether intervening should or should not occur.

BYSTANDERS: IN BETWEEN A
BULLYING ROCK AND A HARD PLACE

To effectively ply their craft, bullies need an audience. They typically feed off the attention of bystanders and attending peers who play critical roles in the process.[1] Many bystanders are unaware that by their presence they instigate, support, elevate, or exacerbate the actions of a bully.

Bystanders are also perplexed about the consequences of intervening to stop bullying or how to reduce the probability of such actions. They may simply choose to ignore the occurrence. Truth be known, a lot of bystanders to bullying incidents are caught between a mental rock and a hard place. For example, although a typical bullying incident involves bystanders (draws a crowd), research shows that 90 percent of children report that bullying is "somewhat" or "very unpleasant" to watch.[2]

Despite most bystanders feeling uncomfortable witnessiing the act, Olweus argues that arousal levels increase when watching bullying and that the increased arousal adds to involvement of children usually not aggressive.[3] In other words, bystanders just don't know which way to go. In reflection, most bystanders are clear about one thing—inaction provides an audience that fuels the bully.[4] This is certainly affirmed by bullies, who routinely interpret the presence of bystanders as a tacit approval of their behaviors.[5]

Other research paints a deeper picture of bystander confusion. For example, one study found 33 percent of students who reported witnessing bullying stated that they failed to intervene but thought they should have.[6] Craig and Pepler also find that peers were respectful to the bully in 74 percent of bullying episodes and only respectful to the victim in 23 percent of the situations.[7] So where does this lead us?

The message seems clear. Bystanders who view acts of bullying experience a wide gamut of emotions. To be effective at eliminating campus bullying through engaged bystanders, trained school personnel must address the emotions experienced by them, reconcile the effects through education and well-articulated anti-bullying policies, and replace role ambiguity with clarity. These are tall orders that can be achieved through highly organized and informed school and community anti-bullying efforts, but certain legal and psychological barriers challenge these goals.

COURTROOM VERSUS CLASSROOM: THE RULE OF LAW AND SCHOOL DISTRICT POLICIES

One obscure but important conundrum associated with bystanders and their reactions to bullying lies in the area of legal liability. Specifically, there is a disconnect between laws governing private citizens and their rights to aid a person under attack, and school board policies designed to protect students from campus violence. For example, in many communities, "defense of third party" laws permit private citizens to defend another person who is being attacked. Third party defense involves the rights of private citizens to respond with like force necessary to protect fellow citizens from an attacker's harm and has a long-standing history of court approval. Previously known as the "alter ego" rule, the right of a third person to protect another is firmly established in American jurisprudence.

In direct conflict with "defense of third party" laws, many public school districts have adopted policies whereby any person involved in a physical altercation on campus is designated a "willing combatant." Under a "willing combatant" policy, anyone who physically intervenes in a bullying situation in attempt to protect the victim potentially could be punished to the same extent as the perpetrator (bully). Obviously, this situation poses a dilemma for both school leaders attempting to combat bullying and bystanders who might be willing to get involved. It's little wonder that witnesses to bullying become hesitant to act when it comes to physically intervening. But that's just the tip of the iceberg when it comes to bystanders being confused about their roles in the bullying cycle. Other factors that stymie intervention by onlookers such as the principle of "social proof" and the "bystander effect" also come into play.

SOCIAL PROOF AND THE BYSTANDER EFFECT

Social psychologist Robert Cialdini has devoted his professional life to researching the science of influence. In particular, Cialdini's work centers on identifying factors that persuade people to act certain ways or make specific decisions. One of the more pervasive human tendencies that he identifies is what he calls the principle of social proof, which states that "we view a behavior as correct in a given situation to the degree that we see others performing it."[8] In other words, one important way people use to decide what they're going to believe or how they're going act is to observe what other people around them are believing or doing.

Cialdini further identifies two social conditions that enhance the probabilities that people will look to others for decision-making or behavioral clues: uncertainty and similarity. In uncertain or ambiguous situations, the decisions by bystanders to assist others are greatly influenced by how people around them are reacting, particularly if the condition isn't deemed a clear-cut emergency. Enter bullying situations and bystanders.

Many bystanders find themselves observing the situation rather than reacting because no one else is intervening, even when similar others (student colleagues) are present. Basically, no one takes the initiative in intervening in the situation because most bullying situations initially involve a less aggressive introductory phase, which leads to hyper-aggressive outcomes. Hence, ambiguity and uncertainty moderate the behavior of the group since initially it may be difficult to judge the severity of the situation.

Further compounding the problem of bystander intervention is what psychologists call the "bystander effect." Closely coupled to the principle of social proof, the bystander effect occurs when a crowd observes a bullying occurrence and no one reacts. Stimulated by the infamous early-morning murder of New York resident Catherine Genovese in 1964, research by psychologists Darley and Latané indicates that, in situations where there's a single bystander, assistance from that person is more immediate than when there's a group of people involved.[9]

According to their research, two factors discourage group intervention. First, bystanders hesitate to react because of the principle of social proof whereby everyone in the group is watching the reaction of the others to the situation. This occurs because bystanders are uncertain of the seriousness of the situation and consequently wait until others provide social clues as to the possibility of intervention. A second factor that moderates bystander intervention is diffusion of responsibility. In this situation, bystanders simply view the responsibility of intervening as shared by the group. They wait until the group decides to act, which slows (or eliminates) the intervention.

Unfortunately, bullying incidents fit hand in glove with both the principle of social proof and the bystander effect. Bullying is a complex phenomenon layered with ambiguity, and bystanders often are exposed to incidents spontaneously. This provides little time for intervention decision making and promotes default behaviors by both individuals and the group that are predicated on the principle of social proof and the bystander effect. This tendency of bystanders to default is exactly why it's critically important for anti-bullying forces to be proactive rather than reactive when explaining intervention strategies. Without advance training and due to the potency of the principle of social proof, the impacts of the bystander effect, and a general lack of awareness of how to respond to bullying incidents in a timely manner, bystanders will continue to struggle with the emotional consequences of observing such situations.

BYSTANDER FALLOUT: THE EMOTIONAL COSTS OF WITNESSING BULLYING

Bullying extracts a heavy toll on society. In a classic sense, perpetrators and their targets dominate the attention of professionals who are trained to deal with the problems associated with bullies and their victims. There is, however, another more inconspicuous group that is affected by bullying and, arguably, represents the key to curbing the activity. Those who witness bullying constitute a majority on every campus, and this group always outnumbers the bullies.

Bystanders who witness bullying frequently experience troubling emotions that can last long into adulthood. They're also victims, but unfortunately bystanders and the emotional repercussions of their experiences are often neglected in favor of addressing the participants directly involved. Nevertheless, the following effects represent how bullying victimizes bystanders in subtle, but no less devastating, ways than actual victims.

- *Stress:* Physiologically, bystanders who witness bullying experience increased heart rates and tend to perspire. These traits are symptomatic of individuals suffering from high levels of stress and, if left unchecked, can cause increased risks of health problems. Psychologically, prolonged bystander stress caused by repeated exposure to bullying erodes interest in academics and prompts absenteeism.

- *Anxiety:* Bystander exposure to a bullying atmosphere can also produce high levels of anxiety. Situation and area avoidance are common occurrences. Victims become preoccupied with avoiding areas where bullying occurs and oftentimes evade school activities they believe might jeopardize their safety.
- *Fear:* Regardless of the target, bystanders who witness bullying are increasingly fearful that they may be next. The increased tendency for bystanders to look over their shoulders promotes a heightened sense of insecurity that may carry well into adult life. In addition, fear represents the greatest challenge that bystanders encounter in regard to speaking out or physically intervening against a bully. Bystanders fearing such things as retaliation by the bully, peer rejection, embarrassment, or public hazing all account for their refusal to intervene in a bullying situation.
- *Guilt:* As a matter of conscience, most bystanders witnessing a bullying episode know they should do something. When they fail to react, bystanders experience deep feelings of guilt. In turn, remorse over failing to come to the aid of a victim often produces "sidebar" manifestations such as substance abuse and sleep disorders.
- *Identity deprivation:* In an environment prone to bullying, bystanders who witness attacks and consistently fail to intervene develop identity deprivation, or the inability to relate to the victim's plight. In such cases, empathy for the target gradually diminishes to the point where the bystander begins to believe the victim merits the attack.
- *Trust:* Bystanders exposed to repeated instances of bullying suffer greater levels of mistrust and relational damage than those who haven't experienced such exposure. Moreover, there's evidence to suggest a carryover effect due to this phenomenon develops as feelings of mistrust linger well into adulthood.[10]

The ramifications of bystanders who fail to reconcile their emotions with psychologically appropriate actions can be just as devastating as the act of bullying. Factors such as stress, anxiety, fear, and guilt converge to form a dangerous palette of emotions that can negatively affect bystanders for years. At the core of this dilemma is inaction. Whether the decisions of bystanders not to intervene or respond to bullying situations are products of the psyche or mere manifestations of ignorance, one fact stands clear: Bystanders who passively yield to bullies encourage them. Indeed, a bully craves an audience, but not necessarily one that applauds.

GOOD THINGS COME IN THREES:
BYSTANDER INTERVENTION STRATEGIES

Once the anti-bullying team establishes "street credibility" through a highly organized and well-executed program of information and repeated instances of support, many bystanders assume responsibility for intervening in bullying situations. In contrast, some bystander reactions such as encouraging the bully's aggression, spectating, or publicly denigrating the victims were *en vogue*, a new energy of intervention emerges in the form of three specific strategies.

1. *Defenders:* This group represents the most proactive and forceful set of bystanders. Largely stimulated by the moral injustice of the act, it's not unusual for defenders to publicly "call the bully out" and physically intervene in the action. Although bold in their approaches, defenders must monitor their intentions in light of the intervention and not be perceived as exacerbating the situation by their rhetoric or physicality.
2. *Withstanders:* Also active interventionists, withstanders concentrate their efforts toward diffusing the bullying situation. They attempt to divert the bully's attention away from the victim and urge others to answer the call of protection. What withstanders lack in their abilities to physically intervene in bullying episodes is more than compensated for by their capacities to facilitate timely group interventions. Withstanders are very adept at soliciting help from other bystanders.
3. *Witnesses:* Representing the largest group of bystanders, witnesses "know the ropes" when it comes to reporting incidences of bullying. They understand that prompt and accurate transmission of incidents to institutional authorities results in action. Witnesses tend to be natural facilitators and meticulously report facts of bullying incidents in collaboration with other bystanders to ensure the facts are accurately reported.

WHAT BYSTANDERS CAN DO

- Let "sleeping dogs lie" and don't join the bully's audience.
- Be a "hole in the doughnut" and don't laugh at the situation.
- Following the incident, extend a hand of friendship to the victim.
- Smell bullying "a mile away" and stay clear of the area.
- Empathize with the victim and include them in your group.
- Know the difference between encouraging and discouraging a bully.
- Make sure to tell an adult about the episode.

SEE NO EVIL, HEAR NO EVIL, AND
SPEAK NO EVIL: WE CAN'T AFFORD IT!

Dating back to eighth-century China, the iconic "three wise monkeys" caricature illustrates the phrase "see no evil, hear no evil, speak no evil." It is believed that Eastern philosophers ascribed being of good mind, speech, and action to these three mystic apes. In Western cultures, the adage largely pertains to someone who witnesses something but doesn't want to get involved. Consequently, the expression is used to illustrate that people who have seen or heard something negative have "turned a blind eye" to the reality of the situation.

For a multitude of reasons, most bystanders fail to intervene when bullying occurs. They turn a blind eye to the attack and, similar to the three wise monkeys, "see, hear, and speak" nothing. This reinforces bullies and enhances the helplessness victims feel. Bystanders failing to resist, report, or intervene in bullying send the wrong messages to both perpetrators and victims. The bottom line for bullies, victims, and bystanders is always the same—bullying is *not* okay. Through well-articulated anti-bullying programs that precisely address how specific policies affect the bullying triad, all stakeholders are acquainted with the message that bullying won't be tolerated.

Simply cataloging an anti-bullying policy in the student handbook and reviewing it at the beginning of the year is not enough. School authorities interested in eliminating bullying must equip bystanders with precise intervention strategies dedicated to ensuring their safety. After this is done, direct administrative reinforcement must follow as bystanders who intervene in bullying incidents see policies supported by immediate action. This evidence of administrative proactivity illustrates to all stakeholders that the leadership of the school is serious about protecting both bystanders and victims when it comes to campus bullying.

Mark Twain once stated that "courage is resistance to fear, mastery of fear . . . not the absence of fear." When bystanders to bullying incidents are empowered to intervene, complacency ebbs and momentum shifts the school culture from fear to faith. As a result, bystanders are no longer simply "standing by" and witnessing bullying. They are combating the problem due to strong administrative support. Empowered by the steadfast efforts of school authorities dedicated to robust enforcement of anti-bullying policies, bystanders overcome the emotional and psychological barriers of intervention, join forces with them to curb aggression, and confront those who author it.

Facts

Bystanders represent critical, but neglected, links of the bullying chain. Although much attention is given to victims and bullies, bystander effects in the wake of an incident actually influence the social milieu of the campus to a greater degree. Silence and detachment from the situation are the usual reactions of bystanders to bullying incidents. Factors such as fear, anxiety, stress, guilt, and mistrust surface when bystanders witness bullying and default to inaction. However, through carefully crafted anti-bullying training, bystanders can be empowered to act, and the transition from being a "hurtful" bystander to being a "helpful" one occurs. A number of reasons exist for bystanders to resist intervening in bullying episodes, including fear of retribution or ridicule, feeling powerless, feeling of detachment, diffusion of responsibility, ignorance, and lack of adult support. Research indicates bystanders will intervene in bullying incidents if authorities reinforce their actions and support them as rational within the context of the school.

Feelings

While it's logical to direct most of your efforts at stopping bullying when and where it occurs, anti-bullying personnel often overlook the importance of emphasizing bystander training. It's critical for you to discuss the options available to school stakeholders when it comes to intervening in a bullying incident. You need all hands on deck as you educate everyone about your anti-bullying program! Moreover, as administrators and school leaders interested in stopping bullying, you may think that lip service is enough.

You might feel relieved that your responsibility is done once you spread the word. The truth of the matter is that when it comes to bullying intervention, bystanders, and school administration, you pay now or you pay later. Lip service is the father of inaction, and inaction is the brother of apathy. If you don't demonstrate that you care about everyone affected by bullying, others who look to you for guidance will follow suit. A tepid suggestion that *"teachers and students should be proactive"* when confronted with a bullying situation often produces greater organizational damage than a strong directive by producing stakeholder fear, guilt, and anxiety. Remember the expression, "don't start two fires trying to put one out"? That can easily happen if you're lax in consistently and vigilantly explaining proactive intervention options to all school stakeholders! Finally, put some push behind the options! Think about it. With your busy schedule, can you afford the time and effort involved in addressing the emotional repair of bystanders *and* attending to a growing problem of campus bullying?

Facilitation

Your program is in place, the staff is trained, and you're ready for action. Not so fast! There's a large group of bystanders waiting for their marching orders, and it's the team's responsibility to educate and convince them that intervening in bullying situations is both a necessary and safe endeavor. And, yes! We are taking questions and providing timely and definitive answers so there's no doubt that everyone knows the score when it comes to bullying. As a school or team leader, you're pretty used to being in charge of things and solving the problems of others, so be prepared for a bit of awkwardness as you ask students and teachers for them to help you. However, rest assured that feeling will pass and your message will resonate.

Be resolute in your delivery to the group and try not to veer into any "gray area" when responding. Demonstrate that you and your team will react in support of their interventions! Also, circle the wagons around a basic summary of what constitutes bullying; how it assumes physical, verbal, and electronic forms; where to go for immediate adult support; and that it's everyone's responsibility to garrison bullying. Finally, you'll be well served to mock up a situation that involves the aftermath and support parts of the bystander's involvement. This reassures the bystanders campus leadership will validate their interventions and that standing firm in the face of bullying is a safe and laudable activity.

NOTES

1. Craig and Pepler (1997); Twemlow (2000); U.S. Department of Health and Human Services (2001).
2. Charach, Pepler, and Ziegler (1995).
3. Olweus (1991).
4. Craig and Pepler (1997).
5. Smith and Birney (2005); Smith and Hoy (2004).
6. Charach et al. (1995).
7. Craig and Pepler (1997).
8. Cialdini (2009, p. 99).
9. Darley and Latané (1968).
10. Carney, Hazler, and Higgins (2002).

Chapter Seven

Parenting, Bullies, and Bullying Victims

Is Home Where the Heart Is?

"In the homes of America are born the children of America; and from them go out into American life, American men and women. They go out with the stamp of these homes upon them; and only as these homes are what they should be, will they be what they should be."

—Josiah Gilbert Holland, *Titcomb's Letters to Young People*

"We shape our dwellings, and afterwards our dwellings shape us."

—Winston Churchill

Upon returning from a wonderful, whimsical, and frightening set of experiences in the Land of Oz, Dorothy Gale summarized her feelings about her beloved Kansas home to her family and friends by stating, "Oh, but anyway, Toto, we're home. Home! And this is my room, and you're all here. And I'm not gonna leave here ever, ever again, because I love you all, and—oh, Auntie Em—there's no place like home!" Actress Judy Garland's closing remarks in Hollywood's Silver Screen version of L. Frank Baum's classic story, *The Wonderful Wizard of Oz*, invoke heartfelt feelings in many people. The picture of Dorothy's family circled around her bed and expressing various degrees of concern about her condition following an accident suffered during a Kansas "twister" reminds us of the importance of a loving family and a secure home environment.

To be sure, both psychologists and sociologists consistently recognize the benefits of membership in families that provide stability, structure, intimacy, and unconditional acceptance. And common societal axioms such as "There's no place like home," "Home is where the heart is," and "Home sweet home," conjure up images of both affection and safety. However, for some individuals, thoughts of home and family situations present markedly different impressions.

While much of the current information about bullying stems from the phenomenon surfacing in schools, a growing discussion of how a bully's home life, and that of his or her victims, is becoming increasingly relevant to those dedicated to curbing the behavior. The roots of becoming a bully or victim stem from various sources, but relationships occurring at home between parents, children, and siblings commonly predict future actions by both parties.

FAMILY FACTORS AND BULLIES: WHO'S DRIVING?

In this day and age, the question of who's driving assumes far more than asking what person is going to occupy the driver's seat of a specific car and thus shoulder the responsibility for someone's safe travel. Enter the era of the driverless car and the question now becomes far more complex. In fact, car companies are now predicting that computer-actuated "drivers" soon will propel many of us to our homes and workplaces without the added responsibility of personally navigating our roadways. However, technology is nowhere near replacing parents with robotic surrogates designed to ease the burdens of child rearing and negotiating the family "landscape." Put simply, parenting is an extremely difficult job requiring tons of energy, patience, and love. And there are consistent debates about "rights" and "wrongs" associated with the task. In essence, each parent has a specific opinion about parenting.

Parents are confronted with the question of who's driving when it comes to issues of proper parenting and control, and their responses may well affect whether their child becomes a bully or suffers as a victim. Cutting to the chase, parenting styles and a family's home environment directly influence bullying behavior. For example, children who bully others are much more likely to experience home environments typified by less unity, feeling, orderliness, control, and social adjustment fostered by parents.[1] The undeniable fact is the family represents the most important cog in a child's development, and hence parent-child dynamics command much attention in the prevailing bullying research.

Although each person asked to describe their domestic environment and the factors that inhibited or encouraged the development of bullying can certainly conjure up subtle nuances that steer away from the bank of the causal "mainstream," experts do recognize several family factors that consistently emerge and encourage bullying behaviors in children. The following considerations represent an accounting of the most commonly cited family factors associated with bullying.

1. *A child feels rejected or recognized negatively by one or both parents.* If you've ever visited a home where the family dog seems "jumpy" or intimidated by the intense scrutiny of its owners, perhaps your thoughts went quickly to the specific mannerisms and behaviors that fostered the pet's uneasiness. Indeed, pets internalize and react accordingly to harsh tones and critical commands. So do children. It makes perfect sense that children are much more adept than dogs at recognizing disapproval, and parents who both condemn and reject their children face the prospects of fostering bullying behaviors in them.

2. *The family is devoid of emotional support and has no interest in its development.* The leadership consulting business is rife with trendy slogans about getting subordinates to believe in themselves, and creative managers consistently attend to such matters. Savvy leaders recognize that the key to healthy organizational dynamics is emotional maintenance of their subordinates through approval and support. Family dynamics are no different. Parents are the leaders of the family and should understand that emotionally supporting their children will pay huge dividends in curbing bullying behavior. A family lacking proper emotional support structures sets the stage for bullying.

3. *The primary method of child discipline and control is physical.* For over a century, trainers acknowledged there was only one way to incorporate desired behaviors in horses. Physical leverage and sheer brute force were maximized to "break" the spirit of horses and make them subservient. However, new and more humane methods of training horses have emerged with surprisingly positive results.

   Pioneered by trainer Monty Roberts, better known as the "Horse Whisperer," the language of Equus stresses behavioral training through non-physical methods, communication, and cooperation. His now famous methods have literally transformed an industry. Families whose children liberally experience physical responses to problem situations lend themselves to planting the seeds of bullying. In essence, physical responses as the immediate solution to control situations often prompt children to internalize the same techniques for controlling nonfamilial exchanges through overt bullying responses.

4. *Mood-based and erratic parental discipline takes precedence over the child's actual actions.* Transference is a term used by psychologists to describe a phenomenon whereby feelings are unconsciously directed from one person (or thing) to another. Hence, a bad day at the office may result in "Fido" suffering a swift kick when his master arrives home. Likewise, that same "bad day" at the office can result in either transferring residual negativism of the day's events to children when parental discipline is necessitated.

Child situations warranting discipline that require consistency often veer into mood-based situational encounters where a parent's present disposition dictates a disciplinary "flavor of the day." This leaves a family path strewn with uncertainty and members experiencing frustration over inconsistencies. Without question, parents who approach child discipline in a consistent manner devoid of "transferred" emotions reap the benefits of children largely disassociated from bullying.

5. *The existence of parental discord and strife promotes the development of bullying in children.* Author and noted lecturer John C. Maxwell maintains that people do what people see. When things are tense between parents, families suffer. Children see and feel conflict. After prolonged exposure to constant parental bickering and conflict, they associate such behaviors from their role models as normal human responses and internalize similar protocols into their own social repertoires. Thus, a family environment where there is constant disharmony between parents breeds a winner/loser scenario and provides visual testimony that antagonistic mannerisms are acceptable keys to success.

6. *Inadequate bonding between children and parents produces dissonance and disaffection.* It's no secret that inadequate bonding between parents and their children promotes trouble. In fact, throughout the animal kingdom examples of neglected offspring and runts-of-the-litter alienation spell all sorts of health-related negatives including higher susceptibility to disease, physical atrophy, and even premature death.

   Although these dramatic features are somewhat diminished for humans, severe behavioral side effects due to inadequate levels of parent/child bonding can and do produce deleterious results. Most certainly, noted author and theoretician Abraham Maslow identified the importance of proper bonding when he juxtaposed Social Needs (through the actions of family and friends) directly in the middle of his noted Hierarchy.[2]

   Parental bonding with children promotes a sense of emotional well-being. Similarly, proper bonding relates to a child that he or she is okay and appreciated, and instills a deeper sense of connection. Conversely, when parents deprive a child of the bonding experience, unmet needs stymie the development of proper social mechanisms and leave room for the development of inappropriate ones such as bullying.

7. *Social isolation pervades the family unit and it lacks depth and span of outside contact.* On November 18, 1978, more than 900 men, women, and children belonging to the cult known as the People's Temple died in a mass suicide-murder orchestrated by their leader, Jim Jones. People around the globe were befuddled at how this horrific event occurred. How could so many people agree to end their lives? Extensive inquiry into the cult and events leading

up to the massacre answered the question. Isolation of the membership from the outside world, coupled with the participants being consistently exposed to a cloistered reality filtered through the lens of limited social interaction prompted Jim Jones to secure the collective deaths of hundreds of people.

On a lesser scale, families who isolate themselves from routine societal exchanges affect similar "limited" realities for their children by prohibiting the healthy exchange of fellowship with anyone outside the nuclear unit. As a result, perceptions are viewed through a very restrictive experiential lens and become subject to arbitrary family norms rather than those of society. If normative family behaviors conflict with permissible societal actions, the potential for children to develop maladjusted social repertoires such as bullying or victimization exist due to the absence of socially approved cultural exposure.

PARENTING, CHILDREN, RELATIONSHIPS, AND BULLYING: DOES THE APPLE FALL FAR FROM THE TREE?

An age-old axiom about children and the results of parenting known to many involves the expression "The apple doesn't fall far from the tree." The statement implies that children often demonstrate traits that are a direct result of parenting influences. Whether pronounced or subtle, the fact of the matter is that parental actions and child-rearing techniques at home wield considerable sway over how children develop and whether or not they are prone to bullying or being victimized.

It's well documented that the relationship existing between a parent and a child can dramatically affect the child's emotional constitution. In addition, a child's ability to cope, basic capacity to persevere, and capability to resolve day-to-day problems are largely determined by skills and perceptions imparted by parents to their children. Perhaps more important, the absence of proper family relationships radically increases the chances that a child will develop and demonstrate antisocial tendencies such as unprovoked aggressiveness and callousness toward others. These traits are natural companions with bullying. In fact, children who bully are more apt to

- evidence insecure relationships with their parents typified by general parental disregard for the child's emotional needs, recognition, and positive interaction; and
- possess apathetic, uninvolved, and less supportive male role models (fathers).[3]

Akin to the apple not falling far from the tree, children learn behaviors though observing role models and mimicking family member's behaviors. Unfortunately, when a child's role model rests in a family that lacks positive emotions and condones ambivalence instead of intimacy, problems tend to surface. In fact, children who bully report that their families do not grasp nor care about problems other than their own.[4]

Let's face it: Society has changed and so has the family unit. Daily stresses on parents commonly promote short tempers, conflict leading to divorce, and selfish calls for "my space." These and a number of other factors challenge family stability and contribute much to children becoming both emotionally and physically wayward.

ISLAND IN THE STORM: PARENTING TECHNIQUES DO MATTER

As one of the most recognized cooking schools in the world, the Culinary Institute of America (CIA) trains chefs from across the globe in the finer culinary arts. Graduates from this highly prestigious institution are employed worldwide in a variety of the finest restaurants. Likewise, the CIA frequently hosts some of the most accomplished chefs in an attempt to provide the highest level of student training possible.

The institute also offers specialized weekend mini-courses for members of the general public who wish to sharpen their cooking skills. During these weekend sessions, "everyday" cooks are tutored by accomplished experts interested in imparting special skills to the participants via tried and true methods of cooking. These "weekend cooking warriors" quickly learn that special techniques and purported secrets associated with fine dining consist of simple kitchen skills employed consistently over time. In fact, under the careful tutelage of a master chef, amateur cooks learn from the pros that a bit of caring and attention during the preparation of their assigned dishes are what makes an ordinary plate special.

To a certain extent, proper parenting techniques parallel the advice of CIA chefs. Just as the weekend cooking sessions emphasize attention to detail, constructive parenting techniques involve attentiveness to simple factors affecting adult-child relationships. A little attention to proper child-rearing techniques can go a long way toward reducing the chances that a child may bully or become a victim. In fact, good parents, like accomplished chefs, take parenting seriously and put forth both the time and effort necessary to accomplish the task. A parent's child-rearing skills will have definite effects (positive or negative) on a child's behaviors as he or she grows, and factors such as patience, openness, honesty, and respect surface as important parental traits necessary for successful parenting.

Most parents understand that as their children grow, Mom and Dad's expectations will change. Under normal circumstances, early childhood is typified by disciplinary and supervisory skills focused on both physical health and safety, while the child's later years are often characterized by parental communication that encourages rapport and permits his or her decision-making latitude to emerge. However, no matter what stage of child rearing is evident, well-grounded (and well-rounded) children are derivatives of parents who take their responsibilities seriously and pay attention to the little things that matter . . . their kids!

At this juncture, readers might be thinking, "I don't want my child bullying and I am ready to do what it takes to prevent it, but what parenting techniques are out there?" This is a typical response from parents and a good question to highlight. But first, a quick look at the "wrong side" of the parenting "street" is in order.

The research literature is very clear that children who come from families using parenting techniques such as harsh and inconsistent punishment—the "Bad Cop" parent—as opposed to a democratic or "Good Cop" style of parenting, are more likely to bully their peers.[5] In addition, children who bully are more likely to have experienced abusive, ambivalent, and/or condescending parental discipline techniques while growing up.[6] Conversely, children who view their parents as supportive of their independence and autonomy are less likely to engage in bullying.[7] To that end, family experts identify four general types of parenting techniques that either contribute to or detract from the potential to bully.

- *Authoritarian* parents are "my way or the highway" oriented. They tolerate little discussion from their children, are likely to give explicit orders to them, expect immediate and unquestioning obedience, and are unilateral in their approaches to child rearing. Authoritarian parents position their children in highly structured environments and expect instructions to be obeyed. In addition, authoritarian parents tend to have low levels of parental responsiveness, and can lack intrusiveness or be hyper-intrusive according to circumstances. There exists strong evidence that children who come from authoritarian homes are more prone to bully their peers than those stemming from other types of environments.
- *Nondirective or indulgent* parents represent the antithesis of authoritarian ones. In fact, they are much more responsive to their children than they are demanding. Nondirective parents tend to be liberal, lenient, and allow their children "long leashes" to explore, learn, and experience life in

self-regulated ways. In other words, they are more permissive and overly engaged. Although children from nondirective homes possess higher social skills and self-esteem, they are more likely to become involved in problem behaviors, including bullying or victimization.

- *Uninvolved* parents are just that . . . largely uninvolved with their children. They ask relatively little from their children and expect nothing in return. Although they may be both aware and concerned about their child being a bully or being bullied, ambivalence and apathy permeates the parenting environment of the uninvolved home, and as a consequence, children often veer into antisocial behavioral areas such as bullying or become victims.

And the winner is . . . *authoritative* parenting techniques! Considering the four parenting types, children subject to authoritative techniques fare well when it comes to escaping bullying. This is because authoritative parents engage their children in responsive, supportive, and demanding ways. Although authoritative parents are assertive, they are not intrusive or restrictive like many authoritarian parents. Where disciplinary methods of authoritarian parents are punitive, authoritative parents view discipline as a way of nurturing (teaching) and supporting their children to become cooperative and socially adjusted members of society.

In sum, these four distinct parenting techniques reflect whether parents are high or low on parental responsiveness as well as the demands placed on the child. These two factors combined with implementing inherent parental value systems, beliefs, and moral perceptions interface to determine how susceptible to bullying and victimization their children will be.[8]

SIBLING BULLYING: IS MALCOLM
REALLY IN THE MIDDLE?

For a period of seven seasons (2000–2006), Frankie Muniz thrilled audiences as the star of the American television sitcom *Malcolm in the Middle*. The series portrays a family of six that experience both typical and nontypical domestic situations. Muniz's character, Malcolm Wilkerson, represents a normal boy who tests at genius level, which proves to be both a blessing and a curse. Due to his being a "middle child" and also being stigmatized by his intelligence, Malcolm frequently experiences testy circumstances wrought by his dim-witted older brother Reese. In fact, Reese often resorts to the cruelest intentions when interacting with Malcolm. In short, his older brother consistently bullies Malcolm, even though Reese defends him at school.

While *Malcolm in the Middle*'s executive producer, Linwood Boomer, enjoyed immense notoriety and recognition for his highly acclaimed television series, much care was taken to illustrate Reese's sibling bullying of Malcolm as a normal part of the family structure. In fact, sibling bullying is *not* normal or healthy family behavior. Although often overlooked by parents, it can produce both serious immediate problems and negative long-term consequences.

Sibling bullying is a form of domestic violence perpetrated by one child on another. It can surface as physical or psychological aggression. Unfortunately, it's often overlooked by parents or viewed as part of the socialization process designed to prepare children to combat later aggressive actions by others outside the family unit. In truth, many parents disregard the warning signs of sibling bullying or simply consider aggressive tactics by one child relating to another as "part of growing up."

There are definite warning signs of sibling bullying, and perceptive parents reduce the possibilities of it happening by carefully watching the social dynamics of their children. Repeated instances of one child hurling foul insults at the other is a common sign that sibling bullying is occurring. Rest assured that the expression "sticks and stones may break my bones, but words will never hurt me" is a total misnomer. Insults like "You're ugly," "You're stupid," or "No one would ever date you" strike deeply and damage self-worth. Do yourself, family, and local school a favor and address the situation sooner rather than later. It will save you a lot of future emotional triage.

Physical aggression is probably the most recognizable form of sibling bullying. It's easy to hear the commotion and see the scratch, pinch mark, or bruise. And what parent hasn't had a meltdown over their child having a bloody nose? Biting, hair pulling, kicking, punching, pushing, and hitting constitute forms of physical bullying that should never be tolerated. A bit more subtle, but closely related to physical aggression, is the prospect of one sibling damaging or destroying another's property. In the extreme, this type of sibling bullying can actually extend to the abuse of pets in order to hurt the intended victim.

Finally, one of the most insidious forms of sibling bullying occurs when there are three or more siblings in the family and two "gang up" on another. Let's come to grips with this situation. Unless a family is inseparably aligned with professional wrestling and illegal sibling "tag teaming" is the standard, repeated sibling bullying by two (or more) against one can quickly induce victim anxiety and depression. In other words, this is a dramatic situation that can prompt severe consequences if not curbed . . . post haste!

GOOD NEWS: THERE'S LIGHT IN THE TUNNEL

It may seem that the information presented about parenting and home life situations of both bullies and victims is a bit discouraging. In and of itself, many of us know that parenting represents an arduous and daunting challenge, and the prospect of warding off potential bullying behaviors in our children or protecting them from aggression via our chosen child-rearing techniques prompts anxiety. However, awareness of the pitfalls and plusses of a child's home life is more than half the battle in avoiding circumstances where your children become bullies or victims. The good news is that, equipped with the proper information, parents are already on the right track to guiding their families to successful, productive, and non-bullying ways!

Facts

When it comes to bullying, home life matters. The critical cog in determining a child's development as a potential bullying participant or victim oftentimes depends on parenting techniques. While nondirective, uninvolved, and authoritarian parenting techniques open the door for children who bully and are bullied, parents dedicated to authoritative styles provide their kids with the best opportunities to avoid the pitfalls associated with bullying. Moreover, families that lack emotional support, promote feelings of rejection in their children, induce high levels of physical and mood-based discipline, and experience parental bickering leading to an absence of familial bonding and isolation script a powerful press toward their children's involvement in bullying or becoming a victim.

Feelings

We live in a complex and accelerated world. Schedules at both home and school are hectic, and change in a moment's notice. Just keeping pace makes us (family and school personnel) wonder if 24 hours is indeed enough time to accomplish our tasks. And for school personnel, confronting bullying and victimization through the lenses of family structures and conduct seems overwhelming. The good thing about considering all aspects of the bullying problem is that the majority of us working in schools are grizzled parental veterans and acquainted with family situations. In fact, we have survived the parenting wars or are currently engaged in them. Take heart and look forward to grabbing a buddy for your parenting "foxhole"! We all realize that people who share common interests tend to bond more easily, and parents who find themselves embroiled in bullying will be grateful for your willingness to share some time.

Facilitation

It's true that time marches on and the past can't be undone, but armed with a decent amount of relevant information about family typologies and their impact on bullying, current problems can be addressed through the work of committed community parents and dedicated school stakeholders. Thus, with a bit of sensitivity and a pinch of communication, parents of both bullies and victims can be brought into the discussion of how to improve both home and school environments. Be prepared to commence your explanation of bullying problems strategically by tightly orchestrating the early discussions of the subject and maintaining firm control over the meeting's time frame, chronology, and agenda. This will avoid falling prey to any "axe-grinding" soliloquys that can derail the future effectiveness of your group.

NOTES

1. Bowers, Smith, and Binney (1994); Stevens, Bourdeaudhuij, and Ost (2002).
2. Maslow (1954).
3. Williams and Kennedy (2012).
4. Rican (1995).
5. Baldry and Farrington (2000); Espelage, Bosworth and Simon (2000); Shields and Cicchetti (2001).
6. Pontzer (2010).
7. Rican, Klicperova, and Koucka (1993).
8. Baumrind (1991).

Chapter Eight

Bullying and the Community

Tempest or Tranquility

"Small streams of hatred can quickly lead to unstoppable, horrific things, so [people] should stand up to any type of persecution or discrimination, whether bullying or malicious gossip."

—Susan Pollac, Holocaust survivor

"If you are neutral in situations of injustice, you have chosen the side of the oppressor. If an elephant has its foot on the tail of a mouse, and you say that you are neutral, the mouse will not appreciate your neutrality."

—Desmond Tutu

Throughout the night of October 8, 2016, Florida residents anxiously awaited news of the devastation caused by hurricane Matthew. Extended family members and friends of affected Floridians remained riveted to news reports of the incoming blow. During the days prior to the Category 4 storm, ambiguity reigned as both weather forecasters and storm chasers attempted to gather information about the strength, duration, and repercussions of the gale.

To uninformed residents, conflicting views over on-site news media reports of the impending disaster and definitive information from the experts surrounding Matthew prompted frustration. Due to the circumstances, information was inconclusive and vague. Many felt that seasoned weather forecasters were hedging their bets by not providing exact details about how to react to the massive storm and the potential effects on Florida's east coast. Frustration continued to mount as the gigantic storm crashed into the Sunshine State.

Just as hurricanes wreak havoc on coastlines, bullying behaviors dramatically affect local communities. Interesting parallels exist between the events that often surround hurricanes and communities where bullying is unconstrained and accurate information is scarce. For instance, as hurricanes are forming, experienced meteorologists observe telltale signs leading to the development of the storm. Similarly, well-informed school and community personnel have little trouble distinguishing conditions that aid and abet the development of bullying.

Just as in the dilemma posed via disseminating accurate information about hurricanes, the timely transmission of precise information regarding bullying in a specific locality often creates multiple challenges. First, like gauging the impact of a hurricane, measuring the extent of bullying in a community is not an exact science. In fact, as is often the case, it's easier to note the effects of bullying through the social devastation left behind than to gauge where the next point of impact lies.

Second, during the meteorologists' tracking of hurricanes, fascinating visual computer models of the storms are presented. The route of the storm, potential increases or decreases in its intensity, and the epicenter of the calamity can be reasonably predicted. Conversely, bullying in a community often represents a taboo subject of discussion and thus becomes difficult to track. Notwithstanding that well-trained school and community personnel can often ascertain bullying hotspots and potential times and locations where the acts may occur, it's tough to get the message out due to the controversial nature of the subject. Many local citizens pay little heed to professional advice about community bullying.

School and community members who disregard the warnings and advice of bullying experts resemble those citizens who, despite official warnings to evacuate, remain behind to suffer the consequences of the coming gale. Sadly, and unlike the temporary effects of hurricanes, *if community bullying is left unchecked, the social devastation won't subside!*

The effects of hurricanes also can be much more extensive than anticipated. Factors such as storm surge levels, rainfall amounts, and damage from waves and wind can produce protracted and unforeseen hardships for the residents exposed to the hurricane. As a result, most individuals affected by severe storms consider only their immediate circumstances and how to temporarily cope. This parallels communities where chronic bullying problems exist. Individuals (or families) quickly react to incidents of bullying in attempts to extinguish the immediate problems. Rationally, this is done to stem the current activity and arrest further aggression.

However, problems often surface when solving an individual incident does not resonate through the entire community. Due to the inherent complacency caused by the resolution of single incidents of bullying, collective inroads are not made to curb the community problem.

The damage wrought by hurricane Matthew forced many Floridians into previously unknown situations. Communities were forever changed, and new challenges emerged. Issues such as cleaning up the aftermath left by the storm, repairing physical infrastructures, and establishing citizen-based organizations to deal with future occurrences all took center stage. Similarly, in communities affected by bullying, residents are also left with environmental problems. The aftershock of community bullying calls for public acknowledgment that damage has occurred. Psychological triage often is required to ensure that the needs of individuals who have been affected are properly addressed. The community must understand that harm has been done and future bullying will not be tolerated. Finally, the general public must be aware that policies dealing with bullying exist and will be enforced.

Bullying in a local community, whether indigenous to the locality or advanced from the schoolyard, represents an insidious problem, which can lead to deadly consequences.[1] Without question, bullying is not a benign social feature. It is carcinogenic, and if left untreated, it will spread. In schools and communities affected by bullying, local authorities must highlight the problem and marshal their efforts to curb it. Prior to mobilizing the fight against bullying in the local community, authorities must filter both action and awareness by educating their citizenry.

CROSSING BOUNDARIES: HOW FAR CAN BULLYING EXTEND INTO THE LOCAL COMMUNITY?

Although much of this book is dedicated to school bullying and aspects affecting its presence or absence on campuses, trends, characteristics, and demographic factors germinating on the schoolyard can play key roles in the spread of the phenomenon to the entire community.[2] The depth and span of bullying is far reaching, and the repercussions of persistent occurrences on school campuses often permeate a much larger area.

While many local authorities struggle with the concept and garrison their discussions to isolated incidences of school-aged offenders, bullying can and does mutate from a student-level activity to a much larger domain. Although it is true that severe bullying only affects a minority of people, lives are permanently altered in these situations and life pathways are indelibly changed. Bullying in local communities becomes very inclusive, sophisticated, and dangerous, and adult behaviors witnessed by youth may initiate a cycle of misery prompted by such actions.

ADULT BEHAVIORS IN THE
COMMUNITY AND THE BULLYING CYCLE

Almost everyone has heard the expression "What comes around goes around." In a nutshell, that phrase captures the potency of how questionable adult conduct can stimulate bullying behaviors in young people. For example, despite the current clarion call for civility in our society, young people witness a daily barrage of adult behaviors that cut against that philosophy.

Kids carefully watch adults and often are more than willing to adopt aggressive personal behaviors demonstrated by them. Seemingly "innocent" adult behaviors such as pushing ahead to gain a better position in the airport boarding line or preying on respectful motorists by nudging into traffic illustrate to young people that aggressive actions pay off. Moreover, places originally designed for relaxation and family entertainment such as amusement parks and professional sporting events often become testimonies to grossly aggressive adult behaviors as the crowd persists in running, pushing, and shoving to gain an advantage when it comes to participating. Verbal outbursts often strewn with high-octane profanities also have emerged as common adult responses to public issues in both business and professional venues.

The recent protests generated as a result of Donald Trump's election as president by those opposing him serve as an interesting example. Although the presidential campaign of 2016 was, in and of itself, a poor reckoning in terms of adult civility as both candidates resorted to numerous public outbursts and accusations, the urban protests occurring after the election imprinted many with media images that reinforced the idea that it's quite acceptable to become violent if things "don't go my way." As strange as it may seem, the most aggressive, brutish, and destructive adults regularly claim their actions are quite legitimate and represent an extension of their "rights" to free speech. In essence, incivility trumps civility when dealing with their personal preferences, and they illustrate to their kids that aggressive (bullying) behaviors are the way to go.

Youngsters observe adults in society and readily adopt behaviors that seem successful in community circumstances. They are introduced to a cycle that both condones and perpetuates societal aggression. The cycle begins as the community calls for civility but instead assimilates adult demonstrations of uncivil physical and verbal actions, which in turn are parroted by young people in the form of bullying. The cycle is completed when student bullying and other aggressive behaviors by young people are noticed. The community clamors for greater tolerance and civility, but relieves itself of responsibilities to control aberrant actions under the mantle of free speech—that is, until the community suffers some traumatic event such as the proliferation of large-scale bullying or violence.

Communities continue to struggle with questions of individual versus societal rights and behaviors linked to each. Children most definitely learn by example. If they see open hostility by adults as successful social interaction, they will adopt it. If they witness adults in the community disrespecting others, they will act in kind. And if community norms support such behaviors through collective inaction, young people will mimic any and all adult behaviors with total disregard of the outcomes. Although much debate can be generated in communities about what is civil or uncivil behavior, one point remains indisputable. *Adult behaviors in a community that model incivility provide examples for children that form the catalyst for bullying.*

ADULTS, THE COMMUNITY, AND
THE HAIR OF THE DOG: IT CAN WORK

In the English language, the colloquial expression "hair of the dog" has come to mean that alcohol should be used following a night of drinking too much to lessen the effects of a hangover. Thus, taking a glass of the same drink that caused the problem becomes part of the solution. Using a bit of the analogy of the "hair of the dog" and applying it to adult behaviors, the community has contributed to the problem of bullying, and so it is other adults in the community that are essential to remediating the problem.

Incivility and less than acceptable behaviors demonstrated by adults (and witnessed by young people) can be moderated by other adults via organized community intervention efforts that emphasize proper social behaviors, stability, and civility. Highly visible, motivated, and properly trained adults working through local organizations dedicated to reconstituting community standards in favor of civility can reduce the probabilities of youth bullying by publicly exhibiting behaviors that discourage negative and unnecessarily aggressive actions by other adults. In other words, adults in a community concerned with revising unacceptable negative behaviors *can* make a difference in changing the conduct of other grown-ups and the youth they influence.

Who hasn't witnessed the actions of an irate parent dissatisfied with the outcome of their child's youth event? In many cases, the incivility is curtailed by the response of the other adults at the event. Consider the example of a parent who sees his or her child called out while sliding into second base. It's a close call that could have gone either way, but in the eyes of the parent, the outcome is an unacceptable miscarriage of justice. They stand up, scream at the top of their lungs, and hurl insults at the umpire. It's at this moment that community members either keep other adults in check or not. This retooling of the social norms by community members can be as subtle as embarrassed glances from other parents, or as intentional as verbal correction.

People who work directly with youth in positions of authority such as coaches, day care providers, dance and cheerleading advisors, teachers, band directors, and recreation personnel can make a huge contribution to curbing overly aggressive actions by both parents and children. Changing a community and the behavioral standards within requires sacrifices in both time and patience. Reinforcing an anti-bullying message often involves perseverance in light of what will probably be denial by many of the existence of the problem.

Educating members of a community to consistently extend positive messages to both local kids and each other, and acquaint them with the fact that there are adults who will listen to their stories takes time. The goal is an overall anti-bullying strategy coordinated by a highly energized and proactive group of adults in the community who are concerned with civility and are willing to exemplify respectful behaviors.

Community members who shoulder this responsibility ultimately have the opportunity to mold a shared vision about core issues surrounding bullying such as mutual respect, tolerance, and valuing differences. Adults who exacerbate the potential for youth bullying in the community by modeling incivility in their actions truly can be "cured" by a little "hair of the dog" as other adult groups choose to engage them in ways designed to translate more socially appropriate behaviors to young people.

COMMUNITY AND SCHOOL:
INSEPARABLE FROM INTERCESSION AND PREVENTION

On April 15, 2013, during the 117th running of the Boston Marathon, two explosions occurred at approximately 2:49 p.m. EST. With more than 5,600 runners still competing in the race, two pressure-cooker bombs—filled with metal shards, shrapnel, and other objects, and shrouded in unattended backpacks—exploded near the finish line along Boylston Street. Out of the ensuing chaos and confusion came horrific results as three spectators died, including two young women and an eight-year-old boy. In total, more than 260 participants and spectators were wounded and 16 people lost legs as a result of the terrorist actions, with the youngest amputee being a seven-year-old girl.

In the aftermath of the Boston tragedy, police interviews with survivors uncovered no witnesses claiming that the perpetrators, 19-year-old Dzhokhar

Tsarnaev and his 26-year-old brother Tamerlan, prompted suspicion or that the unattended backpacks caused undue anxiety. In interview after interview, those attending the event expressed both shock and surprise that such a horrible thing could happen. Events like the Boston Marathon bombings heighten our collective sense of awareness in public places such as sporting events, airports, and concerts. America is now on guard against unforeseen enemies wishing to assault our traditions and affect our way of life.

Both schools and communities are threatened by heretofore undetected actions leading to pervasive incidents of bullying. Like witnesses describing the events surrounding the Boston Marathon bombings, many local residents (and school personnel) fail to perceive anything in their community that seems out of place . . . until the deleterious effects of widespread bullying surface. To be fair, like the observations of both the spectators and participants of Boston's historic marathon, school and community social patterns usually are not subject to noticeably visible shifts, nor are citizens in the habit of periodically evaluating the local behavioral landscape. Only when bullying explodes on the local scene does the problem demand attention.

Like the tragedy that occurred in Boston, many schools and local communities react to the problem after the fact. However, akin to the resilient actions of the people of Boston after the tragic bombings, well-organized citizen groups working in concert with school officials can turn a bullying incident into a concentrated and proactive effort to prevent future trouble. The message is clear. Boston came back and so can communities affected by bullying and incivility.

School and community bullying can be prevented and the nefarious effects of its aftermath can be avoided if communities work hand in glove with local schools by

- understanding that no school or community is immune from bullying;
- recognizing that oftentimes bullying germinates in an atmosphere of silence because the philosophy of See Something/Say Something has not yet been fully embraced;
- marketing a clear and mutually beneficial message of intolerance toward bullying through all forms of mass media;
- promoting and supporting intervention strategies common to both the school and community;[3]
- educating youth, parents, school personnel, and volunteer professionals in identifying bullying;[4] and
- providing stalwart support of empowered bystanders who intervene in bullying incidents.

***

Through these and other creative measures designed to address bullying, concentrated efforts to control incidences of youth aggression in our local schools and communities can occur. By establishing local school and community partnerships, and via universally recognized programs of prevention and intercession dedicated to combating bullying and incivility, safe spaces for all children are encouraged.[5] Without question, organized team efforts that share responsibility and ownership between the school and community go a long way toward curbing bullying and incivility.

In fact, when it comes to proactive actions to address the issue of bullying, we can't afford to wait. The cost of doing so is just too high! So get the ball rolling by reaching out to a solid core of anti-bullying activists in your community who are dedicated to achieving results through modeling civility and changing things for the better. Along with adult school and community leaders, don't forget to involve youth at each phase of your plan. After all, they have the most at stake!

Facts

What is socially tolerated, accepted, and condoned in a community determines behavioral standards for both adults and children. Consequently, adult behaviors oftentimes model what children view as acceptable. In fact, demonstrative adult behaviors can evoke community norms that withstand the temptations of youth to bully. Conversely, aggressive and uncivil public actions undertaken by adults and witnessed by youth offer fertile examples for community bullying patterns to emerge. Thus, a large part of any anti-bullying effort is found in the presence or absence of "civil" behaviors evidenced by adults in a community. Concerned school and community leaders understand there is no perfect place to live; however, they still strive to work together to plan and organize youth-based activities that lessen opportunities for bullying to develop. Understanding the effectiveness of adult role models demonstrating desired social behaviors to both their peers and local youth through concentrated community efforts simply can't be ignored!

Feelings

Leaders experience constant tensions between their intentions and the application of them. What we think and what we actually do are oftentimes miles apart. It's just the way it is. Such is frequently the case when it comes to addressing problems surfacing in the community that affect the local school. To be honest, there usually exists a considerable communication gap between what occurs at school and what's going on in the local community. However, this doesn't lighten the load that both school and community leaders bear when it comes to issues of civility. Indeed, these issues may add or detract from the specter of student bullying. On the one hand, many school leaders feel intimidated by community "players" and shy away from alliances. On the other hand, many school leaders also form "bunker mentalities" and seek to exclude the "outside" community from analyzing their schools. Whether right or wrong, these and other feelings limit valuable opportunities to interface with potent community forces that can assist in curbing student bullying. So let's confront our feelings, recognize that wary reactions to involving community leaders in our efforts to educate bullying out of the school is pretty normal, and get on with forging productive alliances with local citizens as concerned about bullying as you are!

Facilitation

Raising community awareness of bullying is a daunting task. No less ambitious is the prospect of soliciting assistance from community members to address the problem. To that end, one of the major misconceptions about anti-bullying school and community partnerships is that school leaders oftentimes incorrectly assume their community counterparts are well informed about the subject. This is rarely the case. Thus, proceeding to educate potential community partners about bullying through well-designed awareness campaigns is a critical first step. And doing this is not as tough as it may seem!

There is a wealth of information designed to educate your community about bullying, and it is easily available to your team leader. In addition, trust becomes a key component in any attempt to collaborate with community members, discuss common standards of civility, and forward an anti-bullying school culture. Early "meet and greet" encounters will serve you well in "breaking the ice" and establishing both common interests and trust with vested community members. Also, as your organization gains steam, it might be a good idea to invite local media to carefully crafted mixers. At this juncture, the newly formed team is really ready for action and will recognize that controlling bullying is the responsibility of both the school and community. It's also very important that after organizational momentum is established, leaders of the anti-bullying team consider using the results of a community-wide assessment to gauge impressions of how bullying is viewed, common goals are determined, what determines civil versus uncivil actions, and to what extent local buy-in is evident. Remember, without a way to measure outcomes, it's nearly impossible to determine whether your efforts are successful!

NOTES

1. Zhang, Musu-Gillette, and Oudekerk (2016).
2. Bender and Lösel (2011).
3. Miller (2003).
4. McLaughlin (2000).
5. Espelage (2012).

Chapter Nine

Bullying in the Digital Age

"What has been is what will be, and what has been done is what will be done. There is nothing new under the sun."

—Ecclesiastes 1:9

"Technology has ramped up so much that there are no boundaries. . . . It's so faceless . . . they are free to say and do whatever without thinking about it."

—Carol Todd

Bullying is not new. It has been around for thousands of years and will no doubt exist for years to come. The form it takes, however, does change from one generation to the next. With the advent of technology, cyberbullying has presented new challenges that our educational and legal systems are struggling to keep up with.

In order to understand the challenges of cyberbullying and how best to confront it, it's useful to consider how groups of people have responded to bullying historically. To help with this, we ask you to consider life in Ireland during the Middle Ages. This time period evokes images of castles, local lords, and their serfs who worked the land and tended the livestock. Over 30,000 castles were built in Ireland during the Middle Ages. Some have been well preserved, while others now lie in ruins.

While the design differed slightly from one fortification to the next, a common medieval castle had at least two sets of walls. The outer wall would be between 6 and 20 feet thick. Inside the outer wall was a green space followed by an interior castle keep. Some fortifications had a second interior green space at the center of the fortification. With all of these barricades surrounding green spaces, one has to wonder what it was the locals were trying so hard to protect. The answer in Ireland was livestock—cows and bulls.

Cattle raids from competing clans were commonplace. When an attack was imminent, villagers would herd the cows and bulls as quickly as possible inside the fortified castle walls. Over time, bullying raids/cattle raids became less frequent as property owners' rights were established and bullies were held accountable for their actions. Once order was established, there was less need for solid stone fortifications, so that today most cattle pastures are surrounded by wooden fences, low walls, wire fencing, or lines of thick bushes designed to keep the cattle in rather than to keep the bullies out.

We propose that cyberbullying currently poses challenges akin to the bullying/cattle raiding of Ireland in the Middle Ages. Then, in the absence of clearly defined and enforced law and order, community members came together to protect themselves, building their own fortifications as a community to minimize the damage that could be done to them by marauding clans. Now, the advent of the Internet has created a new communal space, one that in many ways transcends traditional governmental boundaries.

While this new shared space creates many positive opportunities for collaboration and shared knowledge, it also provides a new "pasture land" for predators. In this chapter, we will review some of the most common forms of cyberbullying, consider what laws currently exist to protect individuals from this type of harassment, and make recommendations as to what steps you can take to protect yourself and your community from it.

We begin with the tragic story of Amanda Todd. Amanda was a typical teenager. She liked to go online to chat with her friends, and she enjoyed being able to meet new people online. Here is Amanda's story in her own words:

> Hello. I've decided to tell you my never-ending story. In 7th grade I would go with friends on webcam, meet and talk to new people, then got called stunning, beautiful, perfect, etc. They wanted me to flash. . . . So I did . . . 1 year later . . . I got a message on Facebook . . . don't know how he knew me. It said, "if you don't put on a show for me I will send your boobs." He knew my address, school, relatives, friends, family names. Christmas break . . . knock at my door at 4am. It was the police. My photo was sent to everyone. I then got really sick and got anxiety, major depression, and panic disorders. I then moved and got into drugs and alcohol. My anxiety got worse, couldn't go out.[1]

Let's stop there for a second. Teenagers are not perfect. They make mistakes, just like adults. And Amanda acknowledged her mistake. Unfortunately, as Amanda soon discovered, it's extremely difficult to prevent people from sharing information on the Internet. Once it's out there, the comments you've made, the pictures you've posted, or the screenshot somebody captured while you thought you were having a private chat on a webcam can now be shared with millions of people around the world.

What was even more disturbing for Amanda was that the individual who chose to capture her image was now using it to threaten her by shaming Amanda to the people in her circle of friends. It was at this point that the community could have rallied around Amanda to protect her from this bully. Unfortunately, they didn't. To avoid the humiliation, Amanda moved to a new school. She thought she would be able to move on, but her cyberbully returned.

> A year past and the guy came back with my new list of friends and school. (He) made a Facebook page. My boobs were his profile pic. (I) cried every night, lost all my friends and respect people had for me . . . again. Then nobody liked me. Name calling, judged . . . I can never get that photo back. It's out there forever. I started cutting . . . I promised myself never again. Didn't have any friends and I sat at lunch alone. So I moved schools again.

What if this was happening to you or to someone you cared about? How would you respond? One of the terrifying realities about cyberbullying is that the line between virtual reality and face-to-face encounters is permeable. In Amanda's example, the individual who was bullying her online was sharing information with people with whom Amanda interacted face-to-face on a daily basis. That combination can be very powerful, making victims feel as if there is no safe place left for them. That is what happened to Amanda:

> Everything was better even though I still sat alone at lunch in the library every day. After a month I started talking to an old guy friend. We texted and he started to say he liked me. (He) led me on. He had a girlfriend. Then he said come over, my gf's on vacation. So I did a huge mistake. He hooked up with me. I thought he liked me. One week later I get a text—get out of your school. His girlfriend and 15 others came including (the boyfriend). The girl and two others said look around nobody likes you in front of my new school (50) people. A guy then yelled just punch her already, so she did. She threw me to the ground (and) punched me several times. Kids filmed it. I was all alone and left on the ground. I felt like a joke in this world. I thought nobody deserves this. I was alone.

As Amanda's two worlds collided, bystanders once again had an opportunity to get involved. In this case, they did—to her detriment. By yelling out "punch her already," and by filming the incident, the bystanders were encouraging the tormentor's actions, leaving Amanda to fend for herself. Alone. In her own words:

I just went and layed in a ditch and my dad found me. I wanted to die so bad when he brought me home I drank bleach. It killed me inside and I thought I was gonna actully die. Ambulence came and brought me to the hospital and flushed me. After I got home all I saw was on Facebook—she deserved it, did you wash the mud out of your hair? I hope she's dead. Nobody cared. My anxiety is horrible now . . . constantly cutting. I'm really depressed. I'm on antideppresants now and councelling and a month ago this summer I overdosed in hospital for 2 days. I'm stuck . . . what's left of me now . . . nothing stops. I have nobody. I need someone.

Tragically, Amanda did not find the help she was looking for. A few months after posting this plea for help on YouTube, Amanda Todd took her own life. Her mother, Carol, had this to say about the role cyberbullying had played in her daughter's death: "Technology has ramped up so much that there are no boundaries. . . . It's so faceless . . . they are free to say and do whatever without thinking about it." Technology has advanced so rapidly that it's easy to become overwhelmed by the challenges of cyberbullying. Increasing public knowledge about this topic is an important first step in changing the situation so that the next victim is better protected.

DEFINITION OF CYBERBULLYING

According to the Centers for Disease Control and Prevention, *cyberbullying* is bullying that occurs through e-mail, a chat room, instant messaging, a website, text messaging, videos, or pictures posted on websites or sent through cell phones.[2] Hinduja and Patchin have a slightly broader definition, in which they identify the term *cyberbullying* as willful and repeated harm inflicted through the use of computers, cell phones, or other electronic devices.[3]

The problem is pervasive. Approximately 27 percent of teenagers report they have been the victim of cyberbullying at some point in their lives, and 16 percent of high school students report having being cyberbullied within the previous year.[4] In the majority of cyberbullying cases, victims know their bullies, often from school.[5] This fact poses a dual problem because victims often feel as if there is nowhere for them to go to escape their bully.

Interestingly, females are more likely than males to be involved in cyberbullying either as victims or perpetrators.[6] In a study of 4,378 respondents, 16.6 percent of males and 25.1 percent of females admitted to bullying someone else online at some point in their lifetime.[7] Cyberbullying is changing the landscape of bullying. No longer focused primarily on physical violence, cyberbullies use a wide array of psychological techniques to intimidate their victims.

There are many different types of cyberbullying, including the following:

- *Impersonation:* The bully impersonates the victim or impersonates someone else in order to manipulate the victim.
- *Trolling:* The bully posts material that is specifically designed to incite others to become upset. In trolling, the bully does not necessarily target a specific victim but is posting inflammatory comments in order to see who will take the bait.
- *Flaming:* Similar to trolling, flaming is the intentional posting of inflammatory material designed to provoke a reaction from others. Flaming can either be targeted at a specific victim or a general audience.
- *Libel/Slander:* The bully states or writes false information about the victim (examples include falsified images or statements).
- *Shaming:* The bully distributes information that the victim may not have been ready or wanting to share (this can include the unwanted forwarding of sexually explicit images, slut shaming, fat shaming, or information regarding gender identity).

Impersonation

The anonymity of the Internet provides a veil behind which individuals can pretend to be whomever they would like. An online posting by a 13-year-old girl from Canada could in fact be written by a 57-year-old man in Norway. The friend request coming from a 15-year-old boy in California could be a trap being set by the girl who lives across the street trying to find out embarrassing information she can share about you at school.

Alternatively, cyberbullies may choose to impersonate you. By taking your name and profile picture, a cyberbully can then write whatever hurtful comments they please, leaving readers with the impression that you were the one responsible. While these examples may sound far-fetched, they are becoming more and more commonplace. Perhaps the most famous example of online impersonation was the example of Lori Drew. Mrs. Drew, age 49, decided to create an online profile in which she posed as a 16-year-old boy. In her online profile, Mrs. Drew posted a picture of a teenage boy. She created a fake name and a background story that he was homeschooled and had just moved in to the neighboring town, but didn't yet have a phone.

The target of Lori Drew's deception was a 13-year-old girl named Megan. Even though her pictures show a smiling prototypical 13-year-old cheerleader, her parents said she struggled with her body image and told them she sometimes thought about suicide. Worried about "mean kids" at school, her parents moved Megan to a private school with uniforms, hoping it would be easier for her to fit in. Little did they know the real danger to Megan was not mean or aggressive kids, but from the mother of one of their daughter's friends.

Lori Drew listened as her daughter Sarah told her that she and Megan were no longer friends. Sarah claimed both she and Megan said mean things to each other, and Sarah was clearly upset. At that juncture, Sarah's mother hatched the perfect plan for revenge. Mrs. Drew established an e-mail account on a popular social networking site, under the guise of a teenage boy named "Josh." Over the next several months, "Josh" befriended Megan online. With a teenage daughter of her own, Lori knew exactly what to have "Josh" say.

Megan clearly developed a crush on "Josh," and her parents reported that Megan seemed very happy during this time. At this point, Mrs. Drew chose to attack. Under the false Internet identity of "Josh," she communicated to Sarah that they could no longer be friends because he had found out that Megan was a mean person. Lori Drew communicated to Megan: "Everybody in O'Fallon knows who you are. You are a bad person and everybody hates you. Have a shitty rest of your life. The world would be a better place without you."[8]

To a teenage girl who already struggled with low self-esteem, these words were crushing. Her final communication to "Josh" read, "You're the kind of boy a girl would kill herself over."[9] Twenty minutes later, Megan ended her life. Her parents found her hung by a belt in her closet.[10] Lori Drew was in attendance at her funeral.

In the fallout after Megan's tragic death, criminal charges were brought against Lori Drew. Although the jury was shocked by her actions and lack of remorse, legal options were limited. The most appropriate charge the prosecution could find was a violation of the Computer Fraud and Abuse Act, but in the final decision of *United States v. Lori Drew* the defendant was acquitted.[11] She was found not to have broken any laws because laws had not yet been written to criminalize what she had done.

As a result of Megan's story, many states have rewritten their criminal codes or adopted new cyberbullying laws to help address this contemporary form of bullying. The Drew case serves as an important cautionary tale. Impersonation on the Internet is very easy. Regardless of the profile information they provide, the person on the other side of the computer screen could be anyone, and their motives could be malicious.

Trolling/Flaming

Nothing conjures up malicious intent quite as vividly as the image of a troll lurking under a bridge waiting for an unsuspecting traveler to pass by. The term *Internet troll* refers to a person who is looking for someone to attack, often without regard for who their next victim might be. For example, if a local sports team wins an important game, an Internet troll might say mean things about the star athlete, waiting to see who will come to the sport hero's defense. When someone responds, they have found their prey. The troll will then launch into attacks on that individual with the sole purpose of belittling/berating them. Internet trolls are looking for anything that will entice others to enter into an argument with them. They then use the anonymity of the Internet to say derogatory things they would likely never say in a face-to-face conversation.

Popular talent shows such as *American Idol*, *The X Factor*, and *The Voice* have provided a venue for hopeful amateurs to share their talents with millions of viewers. Christopher Maloney was a finalist on *The X Factor* in 2012. In this capacity, he knew that he would receive critique. One can only imagine the courage it must take for these participants to expose themselves to critical judges.

Of course, the judges on these shows are not the only ones expressing their opinions of each contestant's strengths and weaknesses. Millions of viewers form their opinions as well, and many choose to share their views online. Sometimes those opinions go too far. In Christopher Maloney's case, an Internet troll using the name Gary crossed the line. Not only did he critique Christopher's singing voice, he threatened physical violence against both Christopher and his grandmother.

Christopher decided to confront Gary. With the help of his local news station, he was able to track down his Internet troll and question why he had made such vicious statements. Gary's response was to apologize, stating, "I done it while the *X Factor* was on. Someone (I was rooting for) is gone, and he stayed, and it annoyed me." He went on to say, "I'm sorry. It doesn't excuse what I did." Gary seemed shocked that someone had found out who he was and that he was being called out for what he had written, saying, "I didn't actually think you'd read it to be honest." Internet trolls often say things online that they would not say in person. For the troll, the only intent may be to spew vitriol in anonymity, but for their victim, those words can hurt every bit as much as if they were said in person.

Libel/Slander

How far do Freedom of Speech rights extend? There is a rich history in the legal system testing the extent of Freedom of Speech. For example, in colonial America, John Peter Zenger was tried for criminal libel after making fun of the governor in the *New York Weekly Journal*. The jury acquitted Zenger and established an important tradition protecting freedom of speech. However, subsequent cases have placed some limitations on this freedom. For example, in *Schenck v. United States*, the Supreme Court limited Americans' rights to speak out in opposition to the government. It was during this trial that Justice Oliver Wendell Holmes noted that free speech does not "protect a man falsely shouting fire in a theater." But where is that line in regard to cyberbullying?

Limitations on online speech are currently vague, creating an atmosphere in which many people seem to feel they have the right to post any statement about anyone at any time, regardless of the facts. An example of this comes in the accusation that former president Bill Clinton and his wife Hillary Clinton were running a secret child trafficking sex ring out of a restaurant. The original Twitter posting that started this rumor said, "MY NYPD source said . . . Hillary has a predilection for underage girls . . . we're talking an international child enslavement and sex ring."

Next, someone posted a comment that the child sex ring was based in a pizza parlor called Comet Ping Pong. Based on these purported facts, Edgar Maddison Welch walked into the pizza restaurant in question, holding an assault rifle, fired it in the building, and demanded that the children be released. Given the facts of this situation, we ask these questions: When were laws first broken in this case? When a shot was fired? Or earlier when a false story was posted on the Internet?

Public figures have come to expect lies about them to be posted on the Internet, but what about your son or daughter? Should they be expected to tolerate lies and malicious statements being posted about them? In a case in California, *J.C. v. Beverly Hills Unified School District*, a child posted mean things about one of her classmates, calling her a slut and other crude names. When the victim showed the online video to school administrators, they decided to suspend the offender from school for two days. The parents of the cyberbully sued the school district, claiming that their child's free speech rights were violated, that regardless of the facts, their child had the right to say these things and the school had no right to punish her. How do you think the judge ruled in this case? We'll come back to this later in this chapter and see if you are right.

Shaming

One of the most pernicious forms of cyberbullying is preying on a victim's own insecurities. If an individual is overweight, then eating/weight/body image becomes the focus of the cyberbully's attacks. If an individual is insecure about their sexuality, the cyberbully may look to expose their victim's relationships before they are ready to go public. This is what happened to Tyler Clementi.

Tyler was an 18-year-old student at Rutgers University. As he left for college, Tyler got up the courage to tell his parents he was gay. Having grown up in an evangelical church community, this was not an easy admission for Tyler to make, and he had not yet told most of the people he grew up with. Once at Rutgers, Tyler's roommate decided to expose Tyler by setting up a hidden video recorder that would live broadcast Tyler having an intimate relationship in his dorm room with another man.

The plan worked. Tyler brought a man back to his bedroom while his roommate was away, the hidden camera recorded everything, and Tyler's secret was no longer his. The next day, Tyler Clementi jumped off the George Washington Bridge, leaving a suicide note on Facebook that said simply, "Jumping off the gw bridge . . . sorry." The causal link between cyberbullying and Tyler Clementi's suicide may seem on the surface to be direct, but from a legal standpoint the connection is less clear. Did the cyberbully intend to push the victim to commit suicide? Could this outcome have been reasonably foreseen? Clearly, the bully in this case knew that he was violating his roommate's privacy in a way that was likely to cause both embarrassment and shame.

Forwarding of sexted images without the sender's permission is another common way that cyberbullies wreak havoc. In some cases, the initial image may have been sent with consent, but the victim did not intend for the image to be redistributed. An example of this is revenge pornography, in which an ex-boyfriend or girlfriend decides that the best way to exact revenge after a breakup is to post pornographic pictures or videos of their ex for all the world to see. This is precisely what happened to Jessica Logan.

Jessica had sent nude pictures of herself to a boyfriend. When they broke up, he sent them to other high school girls. The girls then harassed Jessica, calling her a slut and a whore. Jessica tried to be proactive, appearing on *Today* with Matt Lauer to tell her story so that "no one else will have to go through this again." To some readers, this may seem like an isolated incident, but in reality, sexting is pervasive. In a survey conducted by the National Campaign to Prevent Teen and Unplanned Pregnancy, 39 percent of teens admitted to sending or posting sexually suggestive messages, and 48 percent of teens indicated they had received these messages.

For Jessica Logan, the shame was too great, and two months after appearing on *Today*, Jessica committed suicide. Michael Ferjak of the Iowa Department of Justice describes the problem of sexting this way: "I think parents, teachers, community members—everybody—needs to be talking about this because whether you choose to accept the fact or not it is probably present in your community, and if it is, then some of your kids are at risk."

LAWS ON CYBERBULLYING

Adding to the problem is the fact that current child pornography laws, which were designed to protect children from adult predators, often make no distinction between consensual and nonconsensual sexting. Thus, the penalty is often the same for the minor who consensually shared an image of herself with her boyfriend as it would be for the boyfriend to then forward the images to other minors without his girlfriend's consent. To many, this lack of distinction seems unfair. Brian Alseth of the American Civil Liberties Union argues that laws need to be changed so that cyberbullies who are forwarding sexted images without consent can be prosecuted without also criminalizing their victims.[12]

Another challenge that school administrators face is ambiguity in the law regarding an individual's right to freedom of speech and a school's authority to control conduct in schools. It is the phrase "in school" that becomes particularly difficult to enforce. Cyberbullying frequently occurs outside of school grounds, but content posted on the Internet can be accessed anywhere and the impact can certainly impede a victim's ability to learn. Currently, there is a lack of clarity regarding when schools should or should not intervene when it comes to cyberbullying. Here are some examples of recent cases.

Earlier in this chapter, we referenced the case of *J.C. v. Beverly Hills Unified School District*, in which a student posted a YouTube video berating a fellow classmate, calling her spoiled, a bitch, and a slut. The victim's family showed the video to school officials, who assigned the girl who had posted the video two days of out-of-school suspension. The parents of the cyberbully then sued the school district, claiming that their daughter's free speech rights had been violated. The judge in this case found in favor of the cyberbully, noting that, in his opinion, the cyberbullying that had occurred did not impinge on the school's ability to educate or the victim's ability to learn.

Conversely, in the case of *Kowalski v. Berkeley County Schools*, a judge ruled against the cyberbully, siding instead with the school's responsibility to ensure a conducive learning environment.[13] The Kowalski case is remarkably similar to *J.C. v. Beverly Hills Unified School District*. In both cases, the cyberbully posted inflammatory remarks about a fellow student online. In both cases, the victim reported the cyberbullying to school officials. In both cases, school leaders administered a punishment against the cyberbully. In both cases, the parents of the bully sued the school, claiming an infringement on their right to free speech. The only difference is that the judge in the Kowalski case found the statements were likely to create a disruption of the learning environment, and therefore were not constitutionally protected free speech.

The precedent both judges are attempting to follow is the ruling from the Supreme Court that was established in *Tinker v. Des Moines Independent*

Community School District.[14] In the Tinker ruling, the Supreme Court established that schools could not punish student expression unless it materially and substantially interfered with the school's ability to conduct business. Thus the benchmark seems clear—freedom of speech extends up to the point that it interferes with the learning environment. But determining whether that line has been crossed is still subjective.

So what is a school administrator to do in light of the current ambiguity regarding cyberbullying? We have three recommendations:

- *Be proactive.* Review your school district policy regarding cyberbullying and disruptions of the educational environment. If guidelines are out of date or do not address cyberbullying, ask for a clarification of current policy.
- *Involve others.* When an incident is brought to your attention, involve others in the decision-making process. This may include members of the campus leadership team, a campus disciplinary committee, or central office personnel.
- *Provide evidence.* Make a clear determination as to whether you (in consultation with campus and district leaders) feel that the cyberbullying has interfered with the school's ability to educate. Provide evidence for this finding, and take action as delineated by your school board policies accordingly.

If school leaders don't feel that the cyberbullying rises to the level of interfering with the educational environment, look for other ways to resolve the situation. For example, administrators can use a "stay away" agreement in which both parties agree not to have anything to do with one another physically, online, or otherwise—and that if they don't, then the school will progress to a more substantial consequence such as suspension.

STRATEGIES TO COMBAT CYBERBULLYING

There is a lot that can be done to combat cyberbullying. One strategy that many schools and parents are turning to is the use of anti-bullying apps. These apps are designed to make reporting of incidents easy and confidential. Once reported, it is the school's responsibility to fully investigate and take appropriate actions to ensure that every child is safe and able to learn.

It's also important to limit the amount of personally identifiable information posted online. Amanda Todd's experience provides a visceral reminder that any information individuals share can be used to harm or bully them for years to come. If a student does become the victim of cyberbullying, he or she should avoid engaging with the would-be harasser. Any response the student posts may simply add more fuel to the cyberbully's efforts, no matter how logical the reply.

Next, students should document the words/actions of the cyberbully. Keeping documentation of the cyberbullying can assist with requests to webmasters to block sites, requests to school officials to get involved on their behalf, or with legal claims against the cyberbully. It is absolutely essential that victims report incidents of cyberbullying. This reporting can be shared with multiple groups of people.

First, a student should tell someone who cares about them. Parents, grandparents, siblings, and friends can be invaluable sources of support. Another avenue for reporting is to inform the website where the incident occurred. Webmasters can then remove offensive material or censor users. While not all sites will respond to such requests, some will, making this an important initial step.

Next, if the student feels that the cyberbullying is impacting his or her education, and particularly if the cyberbully goes to the same school, report the incident to school officials, explaining to them clearly how the cyberbullying is impacting the student's ability to learn.

Finally, consider involving legal authorities. If laws have been broken, then criminal charges can be filed. Most importantly, respond. There are people and organizations in place for students' protection. Students are not alone—and they should not feel alone.

Facts

Approximately 27 percent of teenagers report they have been the victim of cyberbullying at some point in their lives. In the majority of cyberbullying cases, victims know their bullies, often from school. This fact makes it imperative that schools accept the responsibility of combating cyberbullying.

Feelings

Victims of cyberbullying often feel as if there is no safe space to escape from their harasser. They can feel alone and helpless.

Facilitation

There is a lot that can be done to combat cyberbullying:

- limit the amount of personally identifiable information you post online;
- avoid responding to the cyberbully;
- document the actions of the cyberbully; and
- most important, don't stay quiet. Report incidents of cyberbullying to your parents, to school officials, to the website where the incident occurred, or to law enforcement agencies.

NOTES

1. Blanch and Hsu (2016).
2. Centers for Disease Control and Prevention (2015).
3. Hinduja and Patchin (2009).
4. Centers for Disease Control and Prevention (2015); Patchin and Hinduja (2012).
5. Kowalski and Limber (2007).
6. Burgess-Proctor, Patchin, and Hinduja (2010).
7. Hinduja and Patchin (2010).
8. Baumeister and Bushman (2013, p. 356).
9. Baumeister and Bushman (2013, p. 356).
10. Steinhauer (2008).
11. 259 FRD 449.
12. Alseth (2010).
13. *Kowalski v. Berkeley County Schools* (2011).
14. *Tinker v. Des Moines Independent Community School District* (1969).

Chapter Ten

Bullying Reduction Strategies

"It is a capital mistake to theorize before one has data."

—Arthur Conan Doyle

"Some of the best theorizing comes after collecting data because then you become aware of another reality."

—Robert J. Shiller, American Nobel Laureate, economist, academic, and best-selling author

This book began with an introduction to the finer points of fishing. We learned that the successful fly fisherman must "match the hatch" by tailoring his/her lures and strategies to the current insects upon which the fish are feeding. So also must the successful anti-bullying advocate "match the hatch" by using mindful proactive, reactive, and responsive approaches to address the unique situation in their campus and community.

This chapter provides a summary of the various research-based strategies that have been discussed thus far. These recommendations are organized into three categories: (1) proactive plans to help reduce the likelihood of bullying before it begins, (2) reactive tactics for those individuals who find themselves confronting an active bullying situation, and (3) responsive strategies for dealing with a bullying situation after it has occurred. This chapter also introduces two new tools for the reader's tackle box: the Hot Spot Map and the Bully Index, which are useful in assessing where and to what extent incidents of bullying are occurring. As you read through this chapter, consider the "trout stream" in which you are currently standing. What are the natural resources that will help you address the hazards in your environment?

PROACTIVE STRATEGIES TO REDUCE
THE LIKELIHOOD OF BULLYING

Become Informed

It's important to understand what protections are available under state and federal law. Some states have recently passed laws that criminalize cyberbullying, while other states have been slower in keeping up with technology. All individuals have protections under federal law. For example, it's important to understand that regardless of the state in which you reside, everyone in the United States is afforded the freedom of speech. However, this speech can be curtailed if it interferes with a school's ability to educate. Having an understanding of federal and state laws along with local school policies is an important first step in beginning a conversation about bullying reduction in your community.

It's equally important to know local policy. This begins with a common definition of the term *bullying*. All school and community constituents need to have a clear understanding of what constitutes bullying so that they can identify it and report it to the appropriate school personnel.[1] Unfortunately, there is no single universally accepted definition of bullying. Instead, you are likely to encounter different definitions depending on what state you live in or which school you are working with. Thus it is vital that all stakeholders have a clear understanding of how their local education agency is defining bullying, and what policies are in place to combat it. This information will be found in school board policy.

Community members are responsible for electing school board members who represent their values and interests. It's the obligation of school board members to establish the policies that define and provide consequences for various types of school bullying. Therefore, it's crucial that school board members review district policy regarding cyberbullying and disruptions of the educational environment. If guidelines are out of date or do not address cyberbullying, clarifications or updating of current policy may be in order.

Campus administrators are tasked with enforcing school board policies with fidelity. It can be highly beneficial for school principals to enlist the help of both internal and external constituents in constructing a plan to implement anti-bullying policies. Many schools already have mechanisms in place for collaborating with school stakeholders such as site-based decision-making teams, campus improvement teams, community liaisons, or parent liaisons. Working with well-trained campus professionals who have earned the respect of both school and community stakeholders is an excellent place to begin a conversation about school safety. In addition, principals would be well served to identify and establish working relationships with available community support agencies.

Create a Caring Community

What is socially tolerated, accepted, and condoned in a community determines behavioral standards for both adults and children.[2] In fact, adult behaviors serve as powerful communication tools imprinting children with community norms. Kids look to the adults in their communities to learn what behaviors are or are not acceptable. When children see adults handling disagreements in a civilized fashion, they learn what is accepted within their community.

Conversely, aggressive or uncivil public actions undertaken by adults and witnessed by youth offer fertile examples for community bullying patterns to emerge. Thus, a large part of any anti-bullying effort is found in the presence or absence of "civil" behaviors evidenced by adults in a community. Individuals who are interested in curtailing bullying should model community norms that set children up for success in the broader society.

Provide a Positive Home Environment

Individuals who have close and positive relationships with their parents tend to report lower incidents of bullying than their peers.[3] However, individuals who experience maternal overprotection or intrusiveness report higher levels of bully victimization.[4] Similarly, children who perceive their fathers as significant role models in their lives report less bullying than those who have low levels of involvement with their fathers.[5] It's crucial that parents create a positive home environment in which the child feels loved but not over-coddled.

The research is equally clear that disciplinary techniques can impact whether or not children are likely to grow up to be exposed to bullying. Children who come from families using parenting techniques such as harsh and inconsistent punishment are more likely to bully their peers.[6] In addition, children who bully are more likely to have experienced abusive, ambivalent, and/or condescending parental discipline techniques while growing up.[7] Conversely, children who view their parents as supportive of their independence and autonomy are less likely to engage in bullying.[8] Parents would be well served to discipline their children without being overly permissive or overly reliant on physical punishment.

Foster Friendships

Relationships with friends provide a crucial buffer against bullying. When social encounters with peers are positive, children develop stress-reducing behaviors. When their early social encounters are negative, the likelihood of them becoming victims of bullying increases.[9] Students who have fewer friends among their peer groups experience higher levels of bullying than students who have more friends.[10] One of the most important proactive strategies that children can engage in to create a bully-free environment for themselves is to include more people in their circle of friends.

Work Together

The most effective intervention strategies are those that involve and are supported by both the school and the community.[11] One of the challenges in creating partnerships against bullying is the reluctance people have to discuss the problems. Bullies, bully victims, and even school leaders can be hesitant to talk about bullying. People interested in engaging these constituents in conversations about bullying need to be prepared to overcome this initial hurdle. By working together and using universally recognized strategies to combat bullying, school and community partners create safe spaces for students to learn.[12]

School officials who take proactive approaches to bullying by working with local stakeholders to identify when, where, and to what extent bullying is occurring on campus hold a huge advantage over those who don't. Some tools designed to assist in collecting this vital data are found in appendixes A, B, and C. Specifically, a copy of the Bully Index, Scoring Key for the Bully Index, and a Hot Spot Map are included as free resources for the use of our readers.[13]

Whether you use these free tools or choose a different way to collect data, it's crucial for principals to gather this information. The best way to find out people's perceptions about bullying is to ask them. Community-wide assessments represent crucial tools in gauging impressions of how bullying is viewed and to what extent it's happening on your campus.

REACTIVE STRATEGIES: WHAT TO DO
IN THE MIDST OF A BULLYING INCIDENT

Bullying may never fully be eradicated. This simple truth does not diminish the importance of bullying reduction; rather, it heightens it. So what do you do if you are confronted with an active bullying situation? This is where the role of bystander takes center stage. To effectively ply their craft, bullies need an audience. Therefore, it's important that individuals refuse to be an audience—if you're not going to get involved or offer assistance to the victim, then at a minimum refuse to be part of the audience for the bully.

The reactions of those who witness bullying can either encourage or discourage the bully. Recall the story of Amanda Todd. When a bully approached her, it began with words. It escalated when an onlooker shouted, "Punch her already." Silence and detachment from the situation are the usual reactions of bystanders to bullying incidents, but this type of inaction will seem like deference to the bully. Even something as small as laughing at the situation can encourage the bully to continue to torment his or her victim.

Bystanders should be mindful of the impact their words/actions/inactions are having on the situation. Many bystanders don't know how to react. Will they be punished by the principal if they intervene? This is a prime opportunity for intervention through education. By implementing carefully crafted anti-bullying training, bystanders can be empowered to act and can become helpful bystanders rather than hurtful ones. Remember that research indicates bystanders are more likely to intervene in bullying incidents when school officials reinforce and support their actions.[14]

RESPONSIVE STRATEGIES: WHAT TO DO AFTER A BULLYING INCIDENT HAS OCCURRED

Take Immediate Actions to Address the Incident

Anyone who knows about a bullying incident should immediately report the situation to school authorities and, depending on the severity of the incident, to legal authorities as well. We know from the research on social proof that there is a natural tendency to assume that someone else will report the incident.[15] It's important not to assume that the victim, the victim's parents, or someone else will tell someone.

When reporting the incident, it's crucial to provide evidence for any action that is in violation of school board policy, or is a violation of the law. Remember that people in positions of authority enforce policy. The stronger the evidence that a policy or legal violation has occurred, the easier it will be for school or legal authorities to take action against the bully. If the incident is one of cyberbullying, it is also important to report the incident to the website where the incident occurred. While not all websites will take action against the offender, many will. These steps can include removing offensive content, restricting the user, or deleting the bully's user account.

School administrators who receive reports of bullying have a responsibility to conduct a thorough investigation. It's their job to collect evidence and administer consequences according to school board policy. If the incident occurred online, the school will have to make a clear determination as to whether the cyberbullying has interfered with the school's ability to educate. If the evidence is insufficient to prove that a bullying incident has occurred, administrators can use "stay away" agreements in which both parties agree not to have anything to do with one another physically, online, or otherwise. Students who violate this agreement will progress to a more substantial consequence such as suspension.

If you suspect someone you know may be the victim of bullying, invite the person to join your group. This doesn't have to be a huge formality; it can be as simple as inviting someone to sit with your group of friends at lunch, talking to someone whose locker is next to yours, or walking with someone from one class to the next. Although friendships should never be forced, teachers and school administrators can request that trusted student volunteers reach out to individuals they feel might benefit from increased peer involvement. The fact is, bullies are far less likely to target someone who is a part of a larger group.

Victims of bullying are operating in survival mode. Each day, as many as 160,000 students skip school in order to avoid the possibility of being bullied.[16] The most important reminder for victims of bullying is to speak up. Refusing to stay silent is a powerful weapon in the fight against bullying. It's also crucial for bullying victims to find a way to be safe at school without putting their own education on hold.

One good way to do this is to avoid bullying hotspots on campus. By considering the time of day or location on campus where bullying is most likely to occur, victims can coordinate with school counselors or administrators to minimize exposure to these bullying hot spots. Most important, it's paramount that victims of bullying realize their own self-worth. If you know a student who is currently a victim of bullying, remember that they are of value and they are not alone. Remind them to speak up. Ask them to tell an adult, a parent, a counselor, and/or a principal what is happening, and if they won't listen, tell them to find someone else who will.

Take Actions to Address the Larger Systemic Issue

Robert J. Shiller, winner of the Nobel Prize in Economics, explained the importance of data collection by saying, "Some of the best theorizing comes

> **FIND OUT WHEN, WHERE, AND TO WHAT EXTENT BULLYING IS OCCURRING ON YOUR CAMPUS**

after collecting data because then you become aware of another reality." Collecting information on when, where, and to what extent bullying is occurring on your campus is essential information that should be collected on an annual basis. Relying on anecdotal information is insufficient. In order to assist with this data gathering, we suggest using the Bully Index, Scoring Key, and the Hot Spot analysis tool, which are provided for the readers' use in appendixes A, B, and C.

Here is how we recommend using these important tools:

Step 1: Distribute the Bully Index (see appendix A) and Hot Spot Map (see appendix C) to all stakeholders. This includes students, parents, paraprofessionals, teachers, counselors, administrators, and any other constituent groups in your school community.

Step 2: Enter the data from the Bully Index and Hot Spot Map into a spreadsheet for analysis. We recommend that you set up column headings for each variable and constituent group as seen in table 10.1.

Step 3: Analyze the data by constituent group using the scoring key found in appendix B.

Step 4: Prepare a report that demonstrates respondents' perceptions of the level of student bullying and teacher protection by constituent group and a representation of when/where bullying is most frequently reported on campus.

Step 5: Share the results of the survey with stakeholders. At a minimum, this should include all of groups that participated in the survey. It may also be useful to invite additional groups to this meeting such as university partners or regional education service center staff.

Step 6: Work with stakeholders to create a plan identifying appropriate next steps based on the data such as increasing adult supervision at bullying hotspots, or providing additional training for teachers on how to protect students from bullying.

Step 7: Repeat the data collection process the following year. Compare the data in order to determine to what extent the bullying reduction plan was or was not successful, then adjust action steps based on the data. This continuous improvement cycle should be repeated on an annual basis. As the data are publicly discussed, everyone is able to work together to determine common goals and set a course of action to ensure a safe school environment.

Table 10.1. Sample Spreadsheet for Bullying Data

	Respondent Role	Campus	Grade Level	Perception of Student Bullying	Perception of Teacher Protection	Hot Spot Time	Hot Spot Location
Respondent 1							
Respondent 2							

Respondent Role: 1=Parent; 2=Student; 3=Teacher; 4=Paraprofessional; 5= Counselor; 6=Administrator; 7= Other

Facts

Bullying is not only a school problem, it is a community issue. As such, successful bullying reduction efforts must involve all stakeholders. It is therefore crucial that anti-bullying advocates become informed of federal and state law, as well as school district policies. When confronted with a school bullying situation, bystanders play a crucial role in either condoning or condemning the incident. Schools can help empower bystanders by providing support for those who take a stand by speaking out against bullying.

Feelings

Victims of bullying are in survival mode. They can feel as if there is no safe place for them and that their torment will never end. Friends and family can provide crucial buffers against these feelings of isolation. Individuals who have supportive parents and peers report far fewer incidents of bullying than their peers who do not have the benefit of these support structures.

Facilitation

The best way to reduce bullying on your campus is to work with local stakeholders to create a customized plan that "matches the hatch" by using local resources to combat indigenous hazards. This process begins by finding out when, where, and to what extent bullying is occurring on campus. No matter how scary the results, it is important to share the results with all stakeholders so that an honest conversation can be had as to why the data exist and what can be done to improve the situation. While complete elimination of bullying incidents may be elusive, there is no doubt that by following the research-based strategies presented in this chapter, schools can dramatically reduce bullying incidents and increase school safety.

NOTES

1. McLaughlin (2000).
2. Twemlow and Sacco (2013).
3. Beran and Violato (2004).
4. Paul (2006).
5. Flouri and Buchanan (2002).
6. Baldry and Farrington (2000); Espelage, Bosworth, and Simon (2000); Shields and Cicchetti (2001).
7. Pontzer (2010).

8. Rican, Klicperova, and Koucka (1993).
9. Conners-Burrow, Johnson, Whiteside-Mansell, McKelvey, and Gargus (2009).
10. Perren and Alsaker (2006).
11. Miller (2003).
12. Espelage (2012).
13. Smith and Hoy (2004).
14. Banyard, Weber, Grych, and Hamby (2016).
15. Cialdini (2009).
16. Van Roeckel (2012).

Chapter Eleven

Case Studies

This chapter includes five case studies. In this section, a combination of both real and fictitious bullying incidents are presented in order to allow our readers to prepare for actual situations you may encounter in your own schools. Following each case study is a section titled "Discussing the Case." We suggest using this section to develop your own thinking and to engage in group conversations with other stakeholders.

Parents may wish to read these case studies and discuss them with their family members. Teachers and counselors can employ these case studies with groups of students to get the ball rolling on difficult conversations. Principals can use the case studies with groups of teachers for professional development to lead group discussions following a book study. Community leaders interested in anti-bullying efforts can use these case studies when connecting with service organizations.

CASE STUDY #1: NEWCOMER

The following case study is based on actual incidents that occurred in Texas in the 2015–2016 school year. As you read about this incident, ask yourself what you would do in this situation if you were the person being ridiculed. What if you were part of the in-crowd?

The future was bright. A family's fortunes had changed due to securing new jobs, a beautiful new home, and the chance to attend a new school. One of the benefits of having two hardworking upper-middle-class parents is getting to live in a nice neighborhood. David's family had recently moved into one of the most established and wealthiest areas in the city. However, as the new kid at school, David wondered about his classmates. Tall, athletic, intelligent, and well liked at his last school, David had every reason to believe he'd fit right in. And at first he did.

Town Heights was an "old money" neighborhood with a fine reputation—an area where many of the families that founded the city had lived for generations. But there was a tendency to look down on outsiders—even outsiders with money were routinely derided for living in "McMansions," which was the term the group used to distinguish newly constructed homes from their own established estates.

Like any school, Town Heights High School had all the traditional student groups—the jocks, the eggheads, the band geeks—but the biggest difference was this school had a lot more rich kids than David's last school. The first few months of the school year passed without much concern. David made several casual friends, connecting with many of them online. The girls seemed quicker to embrace the new kid than the boys, so finding a date to school dances wasn't hard. The problem started when David asked one of the school's most popular girls to a dance . . . and she accepted.

As a result, the "in-crowd" of popular boys, who had tolerated David up until this point, abruptly commenced taunting him. Affronts—such as "Have you seen that Ashley is going out with the new kid?" "Have you seen how his ears stick out? He looks like a monkey." "Why is she going out with monkey boy?"—often surfaced. Due to the increased harassment, David's world quickly changed. The casual friends he had at school were now taunting and disparaging him, and laughing.

The online derision was even worse, with many of the in-crowd pointing out David's small physical flaws and magnifying them with memes and hyperbole to make them seem extreme. His new girlfriend also didn't last long. She soon grew tired of the teasing from the in-group she had grown up with, and she eventually broke up with David. As a result, his friends abandoned him, and the teasing intensified. Remarks such as "Hey, monkey boy, how did you ever get Ashley to go out with you in the first place, you are such a loser," and "If I looked like that I would kill myself," were routine.

As David's plight at Town Heights High School worsened, his parents suggested moving him to a private school. David agreed and anticipated having a fresh start and making new friends. Unfortunately, the in-crowd at the private school was connected to the same social network as the wealthy public school David had just left. To David, it almost seemed like they were waiting for him when he arrived. Familiar taunts like "What's up monkey boy? Got a date to the prom yet?" were consistently heard as were online posts such as "Looks like we finally got that loser David out of our school." "What a loser."

Two weeks after moving to his new school, David took his life. In his suicide note, he wrote about feeling tormented and worthless. To the outside world, the suicide didn't make any sense. David was an attractive student with a bright future. He came from a stable upper-middle-class family. Why would he end his life? At the memorial service, his brother summed it up by saying that few people realize the power of words and the damage that can be done by bullying.

Discussing the Case

1. What could the school have done to help stop the bullying before it even began?
2. What (if anything) do you think David's parents could have done differently to have avoided the difficulty?
3. What actions on the part of David's friends, family, or school officials could have made a difference once the bullying started?
4. Finally, consider the story from the perspective of one of the bystanders. Imagine you were part of the in-crowd and that while you had not actively participated in the bullying, you hadn't done anything to stop it either. What impact do you think this event would have on you?

CASE STUDY #2: PROBLEM . . . WHAT PROBLEM?

After suffering repeated racial slurs and verbal threats, two students at Blackhawk High School in Beaver Falls, Pennsylvania, reported to their administration that they were being bullied. Shortly thereafter, when the school authorities failed to respond to the accusations, the girls' parents complained to the administration. Subsequently, the administration indicated there was nothing they could do and no action was taken. Several days later, one of the girls who had made the initial accusations was physically assaulted.

Because the school had a zero tolerance policy, and because the victim pushed her assailant off of her during the attack, the school administrator gave her the same three-day suspension that was given to the attacker. However, the situation went from bad to worse as the bullying continued. Eventually, the parents withdrew their children from the school and opted to pay for the costs of private schooling.[1] Unfortunately, no matter what the parents or students did to draw attention to the situation, the school insisted they didn't have a bullying problem.

Facing the possibility of a lawsuit or having to pay for private school tuition may seem like an extreme example of what can happen when a school fails to respond appropriately to bullying, but in reality, there are far worse possibilities. Alexander Betts was a student at Southeast Polk High School in Des Moines, Iowa. According to his mother, he was the subject of intense bullying due to his biracial heritage and his admission of being openly gay. After six months of unending torment by his classmates, Alexander took his own life.

When asked about this tragedy, school authorities refused to address the issue of bullying on the campus. The unwillingness of school authorities to acknowledge the existence of a bullying problem was especially devastating to Alexander's mother. Tragically, Alexander Betts was the fifth student to commit suicide after being bullied at Southeast Polk High School.[2] Clearly the ostrich approach to the problem of school bullying is alive and well . . . but failing miserably!

Discussing the Case

1. Consider the case of Blackhawk High School in Beaver Falls, Pennsylvania. In this case, the school had a zero tolerance policy in place such that if a child was accosted and did not fight back, they would not be punished. However, if they fought back, they were punished as a willing participant. If your child were to attend a school with a zero tolerance policy such as this, would you advise them to comply with the student code of conduct or to fight back? Why?
2. Consider the case of Southeast Polk High School in Des Moines, Iowa. In this case, there were five suicides by children who were bullied within a five-year span. The mother of one of the victims has petitioned the Iowa legislature to criminalize acts of bullying in the state. Are you in favor of criminalizing bullying? Why or why not?

CASE STUDY #3: FRICTION AT UDF?

Located in a beautiful and pristine area of southern Texas, the University of Dramatic Feelings (UDF) is considered the academic "Mecca" of the area. In fact, many in south Texas feel that compared to other colleges and universities in the area UDF is really "the only game in town." After all, the university is known for its wide array of programs, and both undergraduate and graduate students tout the quality of the education they receive. Coupled with the fact that UDF is strategically located in one of the state's most thriving urban environments, the resident population of the campus has doubled over the past decade.

The rapid growth of the University of Dramatic Feelings also heightened the national reputation of the institution, which prompted the employment of increasing numbers of prominent faculty members from across the country. Indeed, the University of Dramatic Feelings seemed destined for Research I distinction, acknowledging it as one of the nation's top higher education institutions. Unfortunately, due to unforeseen circumstances, another even more important distinction soon would be evident at UDF.

Recently, the university hired Ryan Gow, an internationally known professor of social engineering. Initially, the well-recognized scholar was an active and positive contributor to the department, but as of late problems between Dr. Gow and other faculty had surfaced. According to many insiders, Gow's demeanor had changed and frequent complaints about his abusive language and aggressive actions toward a junior faculty member were logged with department chair Alex Flowers. In particular, word had it that Gow often focused his attacks on Dr. Diane Wright, an up-and-coming assistant professor who was both a prolific scholar and a highly respected teacher in the department.

Many faculty members visiting with Flowers were quick to point out that Gow seemed displeased and uneasy with the attention Wright received. Some even suggested that culture bias weighed in on the way Gow, a native of China, dismissed Wright and refused to include her in vital departmental activities.

As a result of the growing departmental turmoil, Flowers tried discussing the matter with Gow but had been abruptly rebuked. In fact, during the conversation, Gow had strongly intimated that he considered the discussion a form of harassment that might lead him to pursue the matter with UDF's human resources department and beyond. Following the conversation, Alex Flowers slowly emerged from his office only to find two messages waiting for him. One was from the provost for academic affairs requesting a return call about Dr. Ryan Gow. The other was from Assistant Professor Diane Wright informing him that she was on her way to the UDF Equal Opportunity Services (EOS) Office. Truly, Flowers wondered if things could get any worse.

Discussing the Case

1. Determine whether the actions of Ryan Gow toward Diane Wright constitute adult workplace bullying. If so, identify the actions to support your decision. If not, what is occurring?
2. From the vantage of a potential victim of workplace bullying and in light of no specific federal laws or policies governing the act, what advice would you give Assistant Professor Diane Wright?

3. Based on Dr. Gow's tacit assertions made during his meeting with the department chairperson, in your opinion what are Alex Flowers's next steps?
4. Based on the message Alex Flowers received from Diane Wright, is meeting with EOS the correct way for her to proceed? Why or why not?
5. If adult workplace bullying is occurring, in your opinion, what are the proper courses of action to be taken by the following:

- Assistant Professor Diane Wright
- Department Chairperson Alex Flowers
- Concerned faculty members who witnessed exchanges between Gow and Wright

CASE STUDY #4: WHAT TO DO WITH UNDEROOS?

The snickers were quiet at first, just a part of the noise as boys shuffled items in and out of small lockers and got ready for PE class, but over the next several days, they would get louder. Almost everyone kept their eyes down, changing as quickly as possible so no one would think they were checking out anyone else. God forbid someone should be accused of being gay. Sam was no exception. He changed quickly, counting in his head—challenging himself to see if he could dress in less than 45 seconds.

The next day the same thing, and the next, only it seemed to Sam that he heard some more laughter—and it seemed to be directed his way. *Never mind*, he said to himself, and continued counting silently in his head—34, 35 . . . right shoe on . . . now the left . . . 42, 43, and done! He hopped to his feet—ready for class. That's when the name calling first started. "Nice hops, Superman!" "Thanks," said Sam, not sure what to make of the compliment—and he went on his way.

At lunch later that day, several more students made strange comments, like, "How's it going, Captain America?" and "How are things in Gotham City?" Sam smiled, gave an answer without really thinking. "Fine, thanks. How's it going with you?" Sam did not realize it at the time, but his choice of clothing, specifically the superhero underwear his mom had purchased for him last year, had caught the attention of some of the other kids in the locker room. This was not the kind of thing that goes unnoticed at middle school.

Sam's father knew that his son was not developing as rapidly as some of the other middle school boys and girls. When he asked his son if he was going to take a girl to the dance, Sam replied, "Nah, I'm not really interested—but there's a new Avengers movie coming out this weekend. Can you take me?" "Leave him alone," his mother replied. "The longer he can be my sweet little boy the better." "I'll be glad to take you to the movies," she said as she smoothed out Sam's hair.

Sam's mother and father had two different approaches to parenting. In his dad's opinion, Sam needed to be more athletic and try to do more to fit in with the other boys. Sam's mom was usually the one to come to her son's defense.

Sam was savvy enough to ask his parents to buy him new underwear, and he now had the same monochromatic garb as everyone else, but the teasing didn't stop. In fact, it was getting worse. Apparently the story had spread across the school, so now everyone seemed to laugh or smile when he walked by. Sam told the PE teacher about the teasing. The coach gave him the option of changing in a private stall in the restroom. Sam explained he had already begun doing this on his own. "Maybe you should stop wearing superhero underwear," was the coach's next pearl of wisdom. "Okay, thanks," Sam said, although he had already made this change as well.

As he walked down the hall to his next class, he heard someone shout out, "Did you see Sam get his first rebound today? He was like the Incredible Hulk out there." Sam heard several other boys laughing. He turned back around to look at his PE coach as if to say, "See—this is what I'm talking about." The coach had a wry smile on his face that communicated to Sam he, too, thought the joke was funny and was trying not to laugh. Sam came to the conclusion that he was not going to get any help from teachers in this school. He decided he would have to gut it out on his own.

This is not a tragic story. Sam did not go on to commit suicide or bring a gun to school. The effect of this prolonged bullying incident was more subtle. Sam became more somber. He asked to stay home more than he used to, and once or twice a month his parents would let him. His grades dropped a little. He had few friends at school because he found it difficult to trust most people.

Two of Sam's other teachers noticed the change in his attitude, and one of them called his parents to ask if there had been any changes at home that would explain Sam's demeanor. There hadn't been, and although the call alarmed Sam's mother, when she asked her son what the teacher could have been referring to, he blew it off saying that the teacher just didn't like him. Most of the teasing stopped after another month or so, although every now and then someone would still make a superhero joke.

Discussing the Case

1. What could have been handled better by the adults in the situation?
2. What is the next best step for a parent who notices this kind of subtle change happening and suspects it might be related to bullying?

3. Can anything be done to prevent incidents like this from occurring, or do you believe that kids will always find some way to pick on one another?
4. What about the bullying victim himself—what could he have done differently?

CASE STUDY #5: PANIC IN PAWNEE

To most residents of Pawnee, McBloom Junior High is the gem of the school district. It's common to hear locals refer to McBloom as a cut above the other schools located in the city. And those comments were for a good reason. The junior high school students attending McBloom are regularly acknowledged for numerous academic, athletic, and fine arts achievements. Both teachers and administrators consistently trumpet the school's successes. In fact, things couldn't have been going better . . . until Mike Simmons arrived.

Midway through the fall grading period, a new seventh-grade student from a neighboring district transferred into McBloom. By most standards, Mike Simmons was an average and inconspicuous junior high school student. Physically, he was of similar build to his classmates, and his early grades measured up quite nicely to the lofty standards set by the McBloom community. Although relatively quiet, Mike went about his business in an orderly fashion and seemed focused on adapting to his new school environment. Mike Simmons was a pretty ordinary student—with one exception. He had a cleft palate.

Upon first transferring to McBloom, Mike was given the typical wide berth that new students experience. Very few of his classmates and teachers acknowledged him. As the new kid ritual unfolded, no one bothered him and he certainly didn't bother anyone. Not that Mike was standoffish, just a bit cautious. All things considered, Mike's school life was progressing well, but that changed the first day back from Thanksgiving break.

Dave Phelps and his group of eighth-grade "band thug" friends unexpectedly happened on Mike, who was having trouble opening his third-floor locker. As Mike struggled with the combination lock, Dave deliberately pushed Mike, who crashed loudly against the wall. "Watch where you're going, Fang!" shouted Dave as he towered over Mike. In an instant, a crowd of students gathered to surmise the commotion and gawk at the scene.

Front and center were Dave's band mates. One by one, they took turns hurling insults at shocked and embarrassed Mike, who time and time again attempted to right himself and exit the hallway. With no teachers in sight and the hallway busy with an audience of anxious students, it soon became apparent that Dave and his crew were not going to relent in their attacks. The more Mike tried to escape, the more precarious the situation became.

Discussing the Case

1. As an immediate observer of the situation, what are your options as a bystander?
2. How do you intervene and *defend* Mike Simmons without becoming physical?
3. How do you and other students *resist* the aggression of Dave Phelps and his group toward Mike?
4. You decide to *report* the incident to the administration. What steps are involved?
5. Following the incident, what can be done for Mike? For Dave and his cronies? For bystanders witnessing the incident?

NOTES

1. Doerschner Calkins (2013).
2. Elmer and Petroski (2015)

Appendix A

Bully Index

	Strongly Disagree	Disagree	Somewhat Disagree	Somewhat Agree	Agree	Strongly Agree
Directions: The following are statements about your school. Please indicate the extent to which you agree with each of the following statements along a scale from strongly disagree to strongly agree. Your answers are confidential.						
1. Students in this school fear other students.	①	②	③	④	⑤	⑥
2. Bullying students is commonplace in this school.	①	②	③	④	⑤	⑥
3. Teachers in this school generally overlook student bullying.	①	②	③	④	⑤	⑥
4. Teachers in this school reach out to help students who are harassed by other students.	①	②	③	④	⑤	⑥
5. Student ruffians in this school intimidate other students.	①	②	③	④	⑤	⑥
6. Students in this school make fun of other students.	①	②	③	④	⑤	⑥
7. In this school, teachers ignore students intimidating other students.	①	②	③	④	⑤	⑥
8. Students in this school threaten others with physical harm.	①	②	③	④	⑤	⑥
9. Students threaten other students in this school.	①	②	③	④	⑤	⑥
10. In this school, there are too many student thugs.	①	②	③	④	⑤	⑥
11. In this school, students intimidating other students is not permitted.	①	②	③	④	⑤	⑥
12. Rowdy student behavior is common in this school.	①	②	③	④	⑤	⑥
13. In this school, teachers try to protect students who are different.	①	②	③	④	⑤	⑥

Source: Smith, P. A., and Hoy, W. A. (2004). Teachers' perceptions of student bullying: A conceptual and empirical analysis. *Journal of School Leadership, 14,* 308–26.

Campus _____ Grade Level _____

Please check the box that best describes your current role on this campus:

_____Parent _____Student _____Teacher _____Paraprofessional
_____Counselor _____Administrator _____
Other (please specify

Appendix B

Scoring Key for the Bully Index

Student Bullying is unprovoked conscious and aggressive action by one or more students intended to achieve physical or psychological dominance over others through intimidation or threat.

Teacher Protection is the extent to which teachers try to protect students from intimidation and bullying.

The Bully Index (BI): The BI is a brief descriptive measure that gauges teacher perceptions of the social milieu of the campus in terms of student-student and teacher-student interactions; it has two dimensions: Teacher Bullying and Teacher Protection.

Reliability and Validity of Bully Index: The BI is a 13-item Likert-type scale that measures the degree to which the students in a school are perceived as bullying other students and the extent to which teachers protect students from bullying. The Bully Index yields two scores—a bullying score and a teacher protection score; the higher the score, the greater the degree of bullying and teacher protection, respectively.

The reliabilities of the two subscales of the index are reasonably high: .96 for the bullying and .73 for teacher protections (Smith and Hoy, 2004). The construct validity has also been supported in a factor analytic study (Smith and Hoy, 2004).

Administering the Bully Index (BI): The BI is best administered as part of a faculty meeting. It is important to guarantee the anonymity of the teacher respondent; teachers are not asked to sign the questionnaire, and no identifying code is placed on the form. Most teachers do not object to responding to the instrument, which takes about five minutes to complete. It is probably advisable to have someone other than the principal in charge of collecting the data. What is important is to create a nonthreatening atmosphere where teachers give candid responses.

Scoring Key: The responses vary along a six-point scale from "Strongly Disagree (1)" to "Strongly Agree (6)."

Step 1: Score all items, except 3 and 7, as:
Strongly Disagree = 1 to Strongly Agree = 6

Step 2: Reverse score items 3 and 7; score as:
Strongly Disagree = 6 to Strongly Agree = 1

Step 3: Compute an average school score for each item—that is, calculate a school average for each item by summing all the teachers scores for that item and dividing by number of teachers in that school who responded to that item. Some teachers occasionally skip items; make sure you divide by the number of teachers in the school who responded to that item.

Step 4: Compute the school score for Student Bullying:
Add the following items: 1, 2, 5, 6, 8, 9, 10, 12. The sum is the school score for Student Bullying.

Step 5: Compute the school score for Teacher Protection:
Add the following items: 3, 4, 7, 11, 13. The sum is the school score for Teacher Protection. The higher the scores, the greater the degree of student bullying and teacher protection, respectively.

Appendix C

Bullying Hotspot Survey

Directions: This is an anonymous survey. Please do not write your name on this form. Responses are voluntary. If you are uncomfortable with a question, please feel free to leave it blank. The responses you provide will be used to help reduce bullying on campus.

1. What time of day does bullying occur most frequently?
2. What month of the year does bullying occur most frequently?
3. Below you will find a map of your school. Please indicate with an X the location(s) where you have seen bullying occur on campus.

(Copy and paste a map of your school here. We suggest using the standard fire safety map as this will be familiar and should be readily available. See Hot Spot Map shown below.)

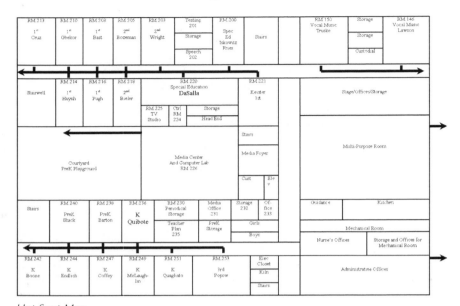

Hot Spot Map

Source: Smith, P. A., and Hoy, W. A. (2004). Teachers' perceptions of student bullying: A conceptual and empirical analysis. *Journal of School Leadership, 14*, 308–26.

References

Alseth, B. (2010). Sexting and the law—press send to turn teenagers into registered sex offenders. Retrieved December 12, 2016 from https://aclu-wa.org/blog/sexting-and-law-press-send-turn-teenagers-registered-sex-offenders

Baldry, A. C., and Farrington, D. P. (2000). Bullies and delinquents: Personal characteristics and parental styles. *Journal of Community & Applied Social Psychology, 10*(1), 17–31.

Banyard, V., Weber, M. C., Grych, J., and Hamby, S. (2016). Where are the helpful bystanders? Ecological niche and victims' perceptions of bystander intervention. *Journal of Community Psychology, 44*(2), 214–31.

Barr, Meghan (2010, October 8). One Ohio school, four bullied teens dead at own hand. Associated Press.

Baumeister, R. F. and Bushman, B. J. (2013). *Social psychology and human nature* (Comprehensive ed). Boston, MA: Wadsworth.

Baumrind, D. (1991). The influence of parenting style on adolescent competence and substance use. *Journal of Early Adolescence, 11*(1), 56–95.

Bender, D., and Lösel, F. (2011). Bullying at school as a predictor of delinquency, violence and other anti-social behaviour in adulthood. *Criminal Behaviour and Mental Health, 21*(2), 99–106.

Beran, T., and Violato, C. (2004). A model of childhood perceived peer harassment: Analyses of the Canadian national longitudinal survey of children and youth data. *Journal of Psychology: Interdisciplinary and Applied, 138*, 129–247.

Blanch, J., and Hsu, W. (2016). Introduction to violent crime on the internet. *Cyber Misbehavior, 64*(3). United States Department of Justice Executive Office for United States Attorneys.

Boodman, S. G. (2006, May 15). Gifted and tormented. *The Washington Post.* Retrieved from http://www.washingtonpost.com/wp-dyn/content/article/2006/05/15/AR2006051501103.html

Bowers, L., Smith, P., and Binney, V. (1994). Perceived family relationships of bullies, victims and bully/victims in middle childhood. *Journal of Social and Personal Relationships, 11*(2), 215–32. doi:10.1177/0265407594112004.

Bump, B. (2016, May 28). Parents sue South Glens Falls schools after bullied son kills himself. *Times Union.* Retrieved from http://www.timesunion.com/tuplus -local/article/Parents-sue-South-Glens-Falls-schools-after-7951546.php

Burgess-Proctor, A., Patchin, J. W., and Hinduja, S. (2010). Cyberbullying and online harassment: Reconceptualizing the victimization of adolescent girls. In V. Garcia and J. Clifford (Eds.), *Female crime victims: Reality reconsidered.* Upper Saddle River, NJ: Prentice Hall.

Carney, J. V., Hazler, R. J., and Higgins, J. (2002). Characteristics of school bullies and victims as perceived by public school professionals. *Journal of School Violence, 3,* 91–106.

Centers for Disease Control and Prevention. (2014). *The relationship between bullying and suicide: What we know and what it means for schools.* Chamblee, GA: National Center for Injury Prevention and Control. Retrieved from http://www.cdc .gov/violenceprevention/pdf/bullying-suicide-translation-final-a.pdf

Centers for Disease Control and Prevention. (2015). Youth risk behavior surveillance—United States, 2015. MMWR Surveillance Summaries 2016; 65(SS10).

Charach, A., Pepler, D., and Ziegler, S. (1995). Bullying at school—a Canadian perspective: A survey of problems and suggestions for intervention. *Education Canada, 35*(1), 12–18.

Cialdini, R. (2009). *Influence: Science and practice.* New York: HarperCollins.

Conners-Burrow, N. A., Johnson, D. L., Whiteside-Mansell, L., McKelvey, L., and Gargus, R. A. (2009). Adults matter: Protecting children from the negative impacts of bullying. *Psychology in the Schools, 46*(7), 593–604.

Cooper, M. A. (2011). New study links bullying to lower high school GPAs— especially among Hispanics. *Hispanic Outlook in Higher Education, 22*(3), 28–29.

Cowie, H., Jennifer, D., Neto, C., Angula, J. C., Pereira, B., Del Barrio, C., and Ananiadou, K. (2000). Comparing the nature of workplace bullying in two European countries: Portugal and the UK. In M. Sheehan, S. Ramsey, and J. Patrick (Eds.), *Transcending boundaries: Integrating people, processes and systems* (pp. 128–33). Brisbane, QLD: Griffith University.

Craig, W., and Pepler, D. (1997). Observations of bullying and victimization in the schoolyard. *Canadian Journal of School Psychology, 13*(2), 41–60.

Darley, J. M., and Latané, B. (1968). Bystander intervention in emergencies: Diffusion of responsibility. *Journal of Personality and Social Psychology, 8,* 377–83.

Dickinson, M. (2010). Research finds bullying link to child suicides. *The Independent.* Retrieved from http://www.independent.co.uk/news/uk/home-news/research-finds-bullying-link-to-child-suicides-1999349.html

Einarsen, S. (1999). The nature, causes and consequences of bullying at work. *International Journal of Manpower, 20,* 16–27.

Einarsen, S., Hoel, H., Zapf, D., and Cooper, C. L. (2003). The concept of bullying at work: The European tradition. In S. Einarsen, H. Hoel, D. Zapf, and C. L. Cooper

(Eds.), *Bullying and emotional abuse in the workplace: International perspectives in research and practice* (pp. 3–30). London: Taylor & Francis.

Espelage, D. L. (2012). Bullying prevention: A research dialogue with Dorothy Espelage. *Prevention Researcher, 19*, 17–19.

Espelage, D., Bosworth, K., and Simon, T. (2000). Examining the social context of bullying behaviors in early adolescence. *Journal of Counseling & Development, 78*, 326–33.

Fentres, A. (2017, February 7). Chip Kelly to Alabama as OC under Nick Saban makes zero sense. Retrieved March 29, 2017 from http://www.csnnw.com/tags/nick-saban

Flouri, E., and Buchanan, A. (2002). Life satisfaction in teenage boys: The moderating role of father involvement and bullying. *Aggressive Behavior, 28*, 126–33.

Goldbaum, S., Craig, W., Pepler, D., and Connoly, J. (2003). Developmental trajectories of victimization: Identifying risk and protective factors. *Journal of Applied School Psychology, 19*, 139–56.

Hanish, L., and Guerra, N. (2002). A longitudinal analysis of patterns of adjustment following peer victimization. *Development and Psychopathology, 14*(1), 69–89.

Hill, J., and Kurtis, B. (Producers). (2008). *A&E investigative reports: Columbine—understanding why.* A&E Home Video.

Hinduja, S., and Patchin, J. W. (2009). *Bullying beyond the schoolyard: Preventing and responding to cyberbullying.* Thousand Oaks, CA: Sage Publications (Corwin Press).

Hinduja, S., and Patchin, J. W. (2010). Cyberbullying by gender. Cyberbullying Research Center. Retrieved from http://www.cyberbullying.us/2010_charts/cyberbullying_gender_2010.jpg

Hodges, E., Boivin, M., Vitaro, F., and Bukowski, W. (1999). The power of friendship: Protection against an escalating cycle of peer victimization. *Developmental Psychology, 35*, 94–101.

Kim, Y. S., and Leventhal, B. (2008). Bullying and suicide: A review. *International Journal of Adolescent Medical Health, 20*(2), 133–54.

Kochenderfer-Ladd, B., and Wardrop, J. (2001). Chronicity and instability of children's peer victimization experiences as predictors of loneliness and social satisfaction trajectories. *Child Development, 72*, 134–51.

Kowalski, R. M., and Limber, S. P. (2007). Electronic bullying among middle school students. *Journal of Adolescent Health, 41*, S22–S30.

Maslow, A. H. (1954). *Motivation and personality.* New York: Harper.

Maxwell, J. C. (2004). *Winning with people.* Nashville, TN: Thomas Nelson Publishers.

McLaughlin, M. (2000). *Community counts: How youth organizations matter for youth development.* Washington, DC: Public Education Network.

Miller, B. (2003). *Critical hours.* Boston, MA: Nellie Mae Foundation.

Mouttapa, M., Valent, T., Gallaher, P., Rohrbach, L. A., and Unger, J. B. (2004). Social network predictors of bullying and victimization. *Adolescence, 39*, 315–35.

Nakamoto, J., and Schwartz, D. (2010). Is peer victimization associated with academic achievement? A meta-analytic review. *Social Development, 19*, 221–42.

Namie, G. (2010). 2010 and 2007 U.S. workplace bullying surveys WBI-Zogby. Retrieved March 29, 2017 from http://workplacebullying.org/multi/pdf/2010_WBI_US_Survey.pdf

Nansel, T. R., Overpeck, M., Pilla, R. S., Ruan, W. J., Simons-Morton, B., and Scheidt, P. (2001). Bullying behaviors among US youth. *Journal of the American Medical Association, 285*, 2094–2100.

National Center for Education Statistics. (2013). Percentage of students ages 12–18 who reported being bullied at school during the school year, by type of bullying and sex. Retrieved from https://nces.ed.gov/programs/digest/d14/tables/dt14_230.40.asp

Olweus, D. (1991). Bully/victim problems among schoolchildren: Basic facts and effects of a school-based intervention program. In D. J. Pepper and K. H. Rubin (Eds.), *The development and treatment of childhood aggression* (pp. 411–48). Hillsdale, NJ: Erlbaum.

Patchin, J. W., and Hinduja, S. (2012). *Preventing and responding to cyberbullying: Expert perspectives*. Thousand Oaks, CA: Routledge.

Paul, J. (2006). Peer victimization, parent-adolescent relationships, and life stressors. *Dissertation Abstracts International: Section B. Science and Engineering, 66*, 56–91.

Perren, S., and Alsaker, F. (2006). Social behavior and peer relationships of victims, bully-victims, and bullies in kindergarten. *Journal of Child Psychology and Psychiatry, 47*, 45–57.

Pontzer, D. (2010). A theoretical test of bullying behavior: Parenting, personality, and bully/victim relationship. *Journal of Family Violence, 25*, 259–73.

Prendergast, A. (2009, April 17). Forgiving my Columbine High School friend, Dylan Klebold. *Denver Westword Post.* Retrieved from http://www.westword.com/news/forgiving-my-columbine-high-school-friend-dylan-klebold-5834485

Randall, P. (1999). *Adult bullying: Perpetrators and victims*. New York: Routledge.

Rican, P. (1995). Sociometric status of the school bullies and their victims. *Studia-Psychologica, 37*, 357–64.

Rican, P., Klicperova, M., and Koucka, T. (1993). Families of bullies and their victims: A children's view. *StudiaPsychologica, 35*, 261–66.

Rueger, S. Y., Malecki, C. K., and Demaray, M. K. (2011). Stability of peer victimization in early adolescence: Effects of timing and duration. *Journal of School Psychology, 49*(1), 443–64.

Seals, D. (2003). Bullying and victimization: Prevalence and relationship to gender, grade level, ethnicity, self-esteem, and depression. *Adolescence, 38*, 735–47.

Shields, A., and Cicchetti, D. (2001). Parental maltreatment and emotion dysregulation as risk factors for bullying and victimization in middle childhood. *Journal of Clinical Child Psychology, 30*, 349–63.

Smith, P. A., and Birney, L. L. (2005). The organizational trust of elementary schools and dimensions of student bullying. *International Journal of Educational Management, 19*(6/7), 469–85.

Smith, P. A., and Hoy, W. A. (2004). Teachers' perceptions of student bullying: A conceptual and empirical analysis. *Journal of School Leadership, 14*, 308–26.

Solberg, M. E., and Olweus, D. (2003). Prevalence estimation of school bullying with the Olweus bully/victim questionnaire. *Aggressive Behavior, 29*, 239–68.

Steinhauer, J. (2008). Woman who posed as boy testifies in case that ended in suicide of 13-year-old. *New York Times.* Retrieved from http://www.nytimes.com/2008/11/21/us/21myspace.html?_r=0

Stevens, V., Bourdeaudhuij, I., and Ost, P. (2002). Relationship of the family environment to children's involvements in bully/victim problems at school. *Journal of the Youth and Adolescents, 31*(6), 419–28. doi:10.1023/A:;1; 1020207003027.

Swearer, S. M., Song, S. Y., Cary, P. T., Eagle, J. W., and Mickelson, W. T. (2001). Psychosocial correlates in bullying and victimization: The relationship between depression, anxiety, and bully/victim status. *Journal of Emotional Abuse, 2*, 95–122.

Thijs, J., and Verkuyten, M. (2008). Peer victimization and academic achievement in a multiethnic sample. *Journal of Educational Psychology, 100*, 754–64.

Twemlow, S. (2000). The roots of violence: Converging psychoanalytic explanatory models for power struggles and violence in schools. *Psychoanalytic Quarterly, 69*, 741–85.

Twemlow, S. W., Fonagy, P., Sacco, F. C., and Brethour, J. R., Jr. (2006). Teachers who bully students: A hidden trauma. *International Journal of Social Psychiatry, 52*(3), 187–98.

Twemlow, S. W., and Sacco, F. C. (2013). Bullying is everywhere: Ten universal truths about bullying as a social process in schools and communities. *Psychoanalytic Inquiry, 33*(2), 73–89.

United States Department of Health and Human Services. (2001). *Youth violence: A report of the Surgeon General.* Rockville, MD: U.S. Department of Health and Human Services, Centers for Disease Control and Prevention, National Center for Injury Prevention and Control, Substance Abuse and Mental Health Services, National Institutes of Health, National Institute of Mental Health.

United States Department of Health and Human Services. (2016). Bullying definition. Retrieved from http://www.stopbullying.gov/what-is-bullying/definition/index.html

Van Roeckel, D. (2012). Nation's educators continue push for safe, bully-free environments. National Education Association. Retrieved from http://www.nea.org/home/53298.htm

Williams, K., and Kennedy, J. H. (2012). Bullying behaviors and attachment style. *North American Journal of Psychology, 14*(2), 321–38.

Zhang, A., Musu-Gillette, L., and Oudekerk, B. A. (2016). *Indicators of school crime and safety 2015.* Washington, DC: National Center for Education Statistics.

Index

About the Authors

Page A. Smith earned his doctoral degree at Ohio State University, Columbus, Ohio. He currently serves as professor of educational leadership and policy studies at the University of Texas at San Antonio. His research focuses on matters of organizational significance where his scholarly pursuits are anchored in three main areas: school climate affecting learning and leadership environments; trust-based organizational change at both the P–12 and university levels; and conceptual and empirical aspects of student aggression and bullying. In conjunction with the aforementioned areas, Dr. Smith has also developed and refined a number of empirical measures that have contributed significantly to both educational practice and theory. He pursues an active role in connecting theory to practice via private consultations, graduate teaching forums, staff development initiatives, and school-community liaison servicing. When he is not engaged in his scholarly endeavors, he locates north of the border and fishes the wilds of Canada.

W. Sean Kearney is associate professor of educational leadership and interim dean of the College of Education and Human Development at Texas A&M University–San Antonio. As such, he oversees educational programming for mental health counselors, aspiring educators, kinesiology majors, principals, and superintendents. Prior to serving as a faculty member and university administrator, Dr. Kearney had the privilege of earning his doctorate from the University of Texas at San Antonio under the tutelage of his mentor and current coauthor, Page Smith. His research interests focus on the areas of principal influence, change orientations, school culture and climate, and the confluence of administration, ethics, and emotionally intelligent leadership.